THE LIFE-CHANGER

The Life-Changer

How You Can Experience Freedom,
Power, and Refreshment
in the Holy Spirit

Francis Martin

REDEEMER BOOKS

Servant Publications
Ann Arbor, Michigan

Redeemer Books is an imprint of Servant Publications especially designed
to serve Roman Catholics.

Most of the Scripture texts in this work have been translated from the
original Greek by the author. Scripture texts that are taken from the
Revised Standard Version of the Bible are indicated by the abbreviation
RSV, copyright © 1946, 1952, and 1971, by the Division of Christian
Education of the National Council of Churches of Christ in the U.S.A., and
are used by permission.

OTHER CREDITS AND ACKNOWLEDGMENTS

In the first several chapters of this work, several excerpts are taken from
Love Song: Augustine's Confessions for Modern Man, translated by Sherwood
Eliot Wirt, Harper & Row, New York, 1971.

In Chapter Three, an excerpt is drawn from *From Darkness to Light,* Ann
Field, Servant Publications, 1978, pages 189-190; material is adapted from
"The Power of the Cross" in the March 1988 issue of *New Covenant*
magazine; material is also adapted from "The Concept of Dying with
Christ" in the October 1989 issue of *The Word Among Us* magazine. Both
these articles were written by the author.

In Chapter Eight, two excerpts are taken from *Hostage Bound, Hostage Free,*
Ben and Carol Weir, The Westminster Press, Philadelphia, 1987, pp. 9 and 89.

Note: the above excerpts and adaptations are used with permission of the
respective copyright owners.

Cover design by Michael Andaloro
Cover Illustration by Jamie Adams

Published by Servant Publications
P.O. Box 8617
Ann Arbor, Michigan 48107

Printed in the United States of America

89 90 91 92 93 10 9 8 7 6 5 4 3 2 1

ISBN 0-89283-661-X

Library of Congress Cataloging-in-Publication Data

The life-changer : how you can experience freedom, power, and
refreshment in the Holy Spirit / Francis Martin.
    p.   cm.
  "A Redeemer book."
  ISBN 0-89283-661-X
  1. Spiritual life—Catholic authors. 2. Holy Spirit. 3. Maritn, Francis,
1930- . I. Title.
BX2350.2.M34555 1990
284.4'82—dc20   89-78216
                                                 CIP

Contents

Preface

IN THIS BOOK, I HAVE TRIED TO DESCRIBE the good news as I have come to experience it in my own life. The joy of this discovery is increased by the privilege of sharing it with others. I wish to express my deep gratitude to our Lord Jesus Christ for having poured out the Holy Spirit and shared with me, in some degree at least, the fruits of his death on the cross and his resurrection from the tomb. Whatever is of merit or profit in these pages is from him. I earnestly pray that he will use this book as a means of furthering his gospel, the good news which is the power of God for salvation for all who believe (see Romans 1:16).

Most of the material in these pages was first delivered orally at several of the annual conferences for priests, deacons, and seminarians held at the Franciscan University of Steubenville. I am glad to express here my gratitude for the generous hospitality and brotherhood I always experience when I am among my friends there. Their encouragement has been loyal and constant.

I wish to thank as well the editorial staff of Servant Publications. In a particular way, I wish to express my gratitude to Mrs. Pamela Moran, a very competent free-lance writer, who undertook to prepare the manuscript for publication. I can only admire her editorial abilities in organizing and adapting for print a series of oral presentations, while ensuring that the manuscript retained the original informal style of my teaching. This book would not have seen the light of day had it not been for her skill and energy.

Though I take sole responsibility for what I have written, it is a joy to acknowledge my debt to my brothers and sisters in the Mother of God community in Gaithersburg, Maryland, from whom and with whom I learned many of the things that I share in these pages.

This book is intended for the general public, for anyone, in fact, who wishes to learn more about the gracious action of the Holy Spirit in our lives. However, I would like to dedicate it in a special way to the bishops, priests, and deacons of the United States, especially those who sat so patiently under the tent during the annual conferences at Steubenville, while I tried to share what I had been learning. May they and all who read this book know the hope and consolation that only the Spirit can give. "See for yourselves, I have labored but a little, and have found for myself great peace" (Sir 51:27).

Francis Martin
Mother of God Community
November 10, 1989
Feast of St. Leo the Great

Introduction

WHO IS THE LIFE-CHANGER? And how can he change *your* life?

Let me start by telling you a story. It is about a man who came to know Jesus. His name was Bartimaeus and he was blind. You can read the story in Mark's Gospel, chapter 10, verses 46-52.

This blind man was sitting by the side of the road, begging. Suddenly, the noise of an excited and expectant crowd aroused Bartimaeus' curiosity, and he asked the people nearby who was approaching. They answered that it was Jesus of Nazareth. Something stirred in the son of Timaeus. Though he didn't know Jesus and couldn't see him, he began to cry out and say, "Son of David, Jesus, have mercy on me!"

He kept this up, even though people were annoyed and told him that he was out of order—that he was crazy to call out to Jesus like that. In fact, "many told him sharply to be quiet." But he kept crying out all the more: "Son of David, have mercy on me!"

Finally, Jesus stood still and said, "Call him." All of a sudden, the attitude of the crowd changed and now they said to him, "Courage, get up." So Bartimaeus, throwing off his cloak, sprang up and came to Jesus.

Jesus said to him, " 'What do you want me to do for you?' The blind man said to him, 'Rabbouni, that I might have my sight.' And Jesus said to him, 'Go, your faith has healed you.' "

That's all it took. Bartimaeus called out to Jesus. Jesus asked him what he wanted and he responded that he wanted to see. He wanted to come out of his darkness, and Jesus granted his prayer.

Straightaway he had his sight, and he kept following Jesus on the way. After Bartimaeus had been touched and granted his sight, he became a *follower* of Jesus. He followed the Lord on the way.

Mark, in telling us this story about the blind man, is really telling us a story about ourselves if we will let him. If we call out to Jesus Christ, he will heal our blindness and make us disciples, equipped to *follow* him.

This book describes what it means to be a follower of Jesus—what it means like Bartimaeus to go back and draw from that initial moment of conversion when the Lord Jesus Christ really changed our lives. It describes the resources, the grace, and the insight by which—in an ever increasing fidelity to the Lord—we grow from being aware of him and his powerful touch to knowing and following him our whole life, until we are received by him into eternal glory. In *The Life-Changer,* we learn *how* and *why* this is essentially a work of the Holy Spirit, accomplished through the power of the cross.

I want to tell you another story. This is a true witness. I will let Leo (this is not his real name) tell the story in his own words. I will comment now and again in order to draw attention to different aspects of Leo's story. My comments will help focus our attention on the working of the Holy Spirit in his life. Read this story slowly. Let the Lord show you how the Holy Spirit, whom he gives to you, can change your life as well.

It had been a particularly dark and stormy night in North Vietnam when my friend and I had gone in our separate fighters, looking for North Vietnamese supply trucks to bomb. Now on the way home, it was even darker. I could tell from the fireball on the ground and the radio chatter that my best friend had just flown—at a speed of hundreds of miles an hour—into the ground and there was no chance that he could have survived.

I was flying back to my own base in complete silence, enveloped in my own thoughts. I realized that my deepest sadness was the fact that even though my best friend had just been killed, it really didn't mean anything to me. It had no effect on me whatsoever. I had become so isolated over the years that I could not even allow myself to feel the impact or to grasp the significance of the death of my very best friend.

I saw this a lot in Vietnam. The immensity of the suffering all around, the fear, the anger, the rage, the insecurity, the isolation, and the death. So many of us, in one way or another, were affected by this living hell. Most of the movies try to make comic book scenarios out of it. Only those of us who were there know what it was like.

ENTANGLED IN SIN

St. Paul, in writing to the Galatians (Gal 1:4), says that our Lord Jesus Christ gave himself up for our sins so that "he could rescue from this present evil age." We will discuss this truth later. But notice how a situation—one that could adequately be described as a "structure of Sin"—created a hellish atmosphere.

Leo will now tell us how he connived in that sinful atmosphere and how it got a deathly grip on him.

I was very young when I began to close off and become isolated from others. I was raised in an atmosphere of physical and verbal abuse. In order to protect myself, I had shut myself off from the normal experience of human emotions.

As my childhood progressed, I slowly became more isolated, more angry, and more fearful. My anger came out in aggression, first on the playing fields at my Catholic grammar school and, then, later on the football field in Catholic high school. By the time I was twenty-five years old and had become a fighter pilot, my aggression was constantly being fed as the military rewarded me for displaying that aggressiveness and that anger in a controlled way.

Notice how early in Leo's life Satan began to weave inextricably together some deep wounds and a pattern of sin. A harsh father beat him physically and abused him verbally, creating in him fear, anger, and insecurity. In turn, Leo reacted against these festering wounds by aggressive and violent behavior. Perhaps it wasn't recognized. Perhaps the violence in our culture is such that his prowess on the playing field was put down to a "healthy manliness" and never seen for what it was. The military was, of course, glad to have somebody who was that willing to be aggressive and violent. After all, that's what war is all about.

All through my Catholic education, I had learned a great deal about God, but I had never come to know God himself in a personal way. I looked upon God the Father in much the same way that I looked upon my own human father. I saw him as an aloof, distant, severe God who always kept score and who would be very quick to punish my shortcomings.

As I grew up, I began a pattern of isolating myself, a pattern that would stay with me for the rest of my life until my conversion. Slowly, I began to pull away from people so that I couldn't be hurt by them, but also I cut myself off from the love that they could have given me. Once I got to Vietnam, all my angers and aggressions were given full rein. After I had been there for a year, I came under the domination of a very powerful, evil force that almost had complete control of me.

I can recall very clearly going to Mass every day when I could, hoping that if it happened to be my last day on earth, my external observance of faith would somehow save me. Yet, internally, I knew that I was slowly being pulled more and more into an anger and a hatred that was beginning to consume me. I remember very clearly going to Vietnam and promising myself that I would never ever attack a village of unarmed civilians under any circumstances.

And yet, as time went by—even though I did not want to do it—I can remember very clearly that by the end of my tour, I had been so taken over by an evil spirit that I purposely and with great premeditation went out and totally destroyed village after village, even if it took repeated missions to bomb them. I could see myself gripped by this hatred. Even though it was a Dr. Jekyll and Mr. Hyde transformation and I didn't want it to happen, it seemed as if I was powerless to do anything about it.

Leo's experience is very common. He had grown up a Catholic. It could have been any other church as well. But he had never come to know the Lord personally. He went through religious ceremonies hoping that they would do some good, hoping that somehow they would provide for his eternal future. Yet as the habit pattern of anger, violence, and hatred grew, he was utterly powerless to do anything about it. Where was the power of Jesus Christ in his life? Where was the gospel, the living Word of God, reverberating in his heart and mind, giving him knowledge of Jesus Christ?

Leo's example may be extreme, but how many millions of people are there who see themselves confronted each day with habit patterns of sin over which they are powerless, even if they are not as violent or dramatic as those which Leo faced? The message from God in our century is the message of good news. God is acting. The Holy Spirit is changing lives, giving people unmistakable evidence of the presence and power of Jesus Christ, who is the Savior of the world.

For such people, the sacraments aren't merely religious ceremonies but personal and communal encounters with the living

Christ. Prayer and reading Scripture have taken on a new meaning and richness. The Lord is giving these people concrete evidence of his power in their changed lives. That evidence shows itself in the freedom from bondage and blindness that they receive as they, like Bartimaeus, call out to Jesus Christ—perhaps not recognizing yet that even this calling out is a work of the Holy Spirit within them.

Now let's turn back to Leo and see how you can have it all and still lack what is most needful.

After Vietnam in civilian life, I strove very hard to repress the anger and resentment that were within me. I got involved in land development and became a very wealthy man. In order to continue my inner isolation, I moved onto a very large, 400-acre piece of property. In the middle of it, I built a dream home for my wife and our children.

Of course, my isolation deepened. I had everything that the world said would make me happy. I had a lot of money, I had a huge house, I had a nice family. But I knew that my isolation and my inability to open myself up to others was keeping me from really experiencing a full and complete family life—a loving relationship with my wife and our three daughters.

As time went by, even though externally I had everything that was supposed to make me happy, I knew that deep inside, all was far from right. The anger, the fear, the resentment were there. At times when I was really honest with myself, I could see despair and even hopelessness. I believed down deep inside that there was an answer. I didn't know what the answer was. Yet, within me, there was an inner voice that said the answer had to be in my faith.

Like the noisy crowd surrounding the blind man, the external practices of the faith at least were bearing witness to a man in darkness that there might be a solution somewhere. Leo knew nothing about it. Yet some inner voice was telling him that somehow in his relationship with Jesus Christ, there was an answer. In his own way, Leo began to call out to Jesus. He probably experienced, both from within and without, the same kind of annoyed opposition that Bartimaeus experienced. How silly to call out to Christ when you're in darkness and don't even know him—how silly to listen to that one tiny shred of witness rather than to the overwhelming evidence of darkness, anger, and isolation.

THE INITIAL MOMENT OF CONVERSION

I continued searching for an answer to the darkness, hurts, fear, anger and hopelessness within me. Then, in my thirty-fifth year, God in his sovereign mercy acted in my life and allowed me to come to know him in a very powerful way. My wife and I had gone on a Marriage Encounter weekend. Toward the end of the weekend, by the grace of God, I had been able to admit to my wife Sandy all the things that I had kept bottled up within me over the past thirty-five years.

There was one point—I remember it vividly—when the Holy Spirit really released me from much of the bondage I had been in. I broke down and sobbed for about twenty minutes. In some ways, I was weeping for all the hurt I had caused others, but also I know I was crying tears of joy.

By the end of that weekend, I knew beyond a shadow of a doubt to the very depths of my being, that I had been healed. I knew that there had been a great, powerful change in my life. I didn't realize at the moment that what had happened to me was the work of the Holy Spirit which had touched my life in such a magnificent and powerful way. But I did go home, knowing that I had been freed from a great weight. It was as if I could walk on air. I felt so free and so unburdened, so washed clean. I know that for the first time in my life, I could really give and receive love in a way that was enabling me to be healed of lifelong patterns of anger and violence. I know that I was able to love my children as I had never been able to love them before. And now I was able to deal with them in a way of compassion and love that I had never been able to show them prior to this.

It would be an error to restrict ourselves to a "psychological" explanation of what happened to Leo. Yes, there was a very deep human experience. Leo was able to share with another human being, his wife, and finally verbalize all that he had kept within himself. This happened to him as he had answered an invitation of the Lord to come aside and spend a weekend on retreat.

Something was stirring within him. It was the work of the sovereign Lord and God who brought Leo on that retreat and used both the sacrament of matrimony and the human wisdom of open communication to begin anew in Leo's life. This was the first touch of God, the first perceptible awareness of God, that had entered into Leo's consciousness.

There may have been other moments (Leo may have forgotten them). But it seems obvious that at this moment, faith in Leo's life began to be something other than acknowledgment that perhaps a certain series of propositions were true. Now it was an experience of the power of God that had changed his life.

As this story unfolds, you will see that Leo continued to be faithful to that grace and so it grew in his life. There are many people whom the Lord touches, but somehow or other, after that initial healing—that beginning of the cure of their blindness—they do not follow Jesus on the way as Bartimaeus and Leo did.

CONVERSION IS FOR LIFE

*Almost immediately after this, my relationship with my children grew deeper and more affectionate. There had been times in the past when despite all my resolutions I had punished them **with physical harshness,** even though that was the last thing in the world I wanted to do. Since that moment during that weekend fourteen years ago, I have never punished them physically. **There has been no need.** I have dealt with them firmly, but I have been able to deal with them by the power of the Holy Spirit—in love, compassion, and with real caring. And they have responded to that.*

Before that weekend, I could sense that my wife and I were drifting apart, even though Sandy had tried very hard to love me and care for me. I was unable to love and care for her. From the moment that God touched my life, our love relationship deepened. Now it has become a great source of strength and clarity, healing and upbuilding, for both of us.

In the same way, I found that I wanted to be with other people of like mind. Whenever I was with other Christians—other people who had experienced the power of God in their lives—I could sense a communication. I was happy to be with them, to love them, and to receive their love. I also experienced in their forgiveness and their acceptance, God's forgiveness and his acceptance.

My whole relationship with my father changed. I was able to reconcile myself with him for the first time in my life. And I was able to truly love him and care for him.

I also noticed that I wanted very much to literally spend my life with other people. I began to think about ways of selling my dream home and moving away from the isolation of the large piece of property that we lived on, so that we could have a house in town and be near our newfound brothers and sisters in Christ. Eventually, my search led me to a Christian community. And that's where I've lived for the past ten years.

When I think of my past life before conversion and how I was so closed off to receiving love and to giving love to others, and when I think of all the many ways that God has revealed his love to me—both inward through the power of the Holy Spirit, and externally, through my relationships with my brothers and sisters—I see how great and merciful and powerful the Holy Spirit is. I see how deeply he can work within our lives to transform us from lifelong bondage, to give us true freedom through and in Christ.

In this part of Leo's witness, we see the work of what St. Thomas Aquinas calls "healing grace." Having once established our life on the foundation, which is Christ, through an initial conversion experience, the grace of the Holy Spirit begins to heal and correct the deception in our minds and the habit patterns of sin in the whole of our personality. We begin to understand reality for what it really is. We are able to understand the word of the Lord as it comes to us through the witness of the love of others. We become enthusiastic about caring in the same way for others. This healing grace is meant to restore to us a basic level of humanity. It is often said that "grace builds upon nature." This is true only of *healed nature.* The shifting sands of the disordered drives within us provide no foundation for the work of the Holy Spirit. You can see in Leo's life the gradual work of establishing within him a basis for furthering the work of the redeeming Christ.

This stage in our conversion is most important. Unfortunately, it is often overlooked. After an initial conversion experience and the beginning of an awareness of the Holy Spirit in their lives, people want to be a "spiritual success." But they do not listen to the Lord as he tries to teach them how to protect the work of the Holy Spirit going on within them. As a result, the work of the Holy Spirit is quenched.

Leo knew that despite all the problems his father had caused him, there was a sin in his own heart—that there was anger and resentment against his father. When he repented and sought reconciliation from his side, the whole relationship began to change. This is part of the work of healing grace. If we neglect or disobey the promptings of the Holy Spirit which lead us to repentance for our share in the disorder and sin in our life, then the healing work of the cross will come to an end and we will never grow into a living knowledge of God.

THE POWER OF THE CROSS

After a year or so in my new home in a Christian community, my wife and I were prayed with for baptism in the Holy Spirit. It was not a dramatic moment in my life. Yet I was aware that I had a new power within me. During the preparatory year, my brothers in the community urged me to apply my mind to the Scriptures and to learn to listen to the Lord as he instructed me through the Scriptures. They urged me to make a fearless inventory of my life and repent to the Lord for all the sin that he brought to mind. I did these things in a prolonged and serious preparation for the grace of being baptized in the Holy Spirit.

The fruit of that grace has been a whole series of healings and reorderings of my life that I know have taken place because the power of the cross of Jesus Christ has been applied by the Holy Spirit to my life and has brought them about. They are for me the living witnesses within my own heart of the love that God has for me and the power of the salvation he brought about in his Son Jesus Christ.

I remember very clearly one of the greatest healings for me. Because of my aggression and anger, I had always been fascinated by guns. I had always owned guns. I had always shot guns. I had always relied on them and their power, and possessed many of them. I recall that even after my initial conversion, I still would take my favorite gun out and shoot it once in a while. However, within just a few months, I couldn't even stand to shoot the weapon. It seemed so violent and so foreign to what was happening within me. I remember very clearly, it was about a year after my conversion, I took all my guns and all my ammunition (I had thousands of rounds of ammunition) and gave them away because I didn't want to have any part of them whatsoever.

After my baptism in the Holy Spirit, this work of being detached from violence went much deeper. I can remember one time late at night, walking along a deserted city street, thinking to myself what I would do if I were assaulted or mugged. At that moment, I heard the Lord very clearly say to me that if someone were to come at that moment and attack me, I should turn the other cheek and pray for the man who did this to me. I began to pray and accepted that directive from the Lord for that moment and for the future.

I was not attacked that night, but I know that something much more significant happened. There was a deep change within my heart. Throughout my entire life, I had always thought about, practiced, and believed that I should strike out and fight back in any and every case. I marvel now to see how the Lord, through the power of the cross, has changed my heart in this regard and given me a deep desire to be a peacemaker.

I know that my attitude toward God has changed from one seeing God as an aloof, stern, vengeful figure to a very loving, forgiving, merciful, and just Father who cares deeply for us and sends the Holy Spirit to be with us at all times. I know that I have been healed of many of my angers and resentments and fears.

When I was baptized in the Holy Spirit, I remember very clearly the Lord showing me an image of myself standing on a dock, which represented my old life, the life that I knew. Even though there were things wrong with it, it was the only thing that I really knew and was comfortable with. And there was a boat leaving the dock. I knew that the boat was going somewhere on a journey, but I didn't know where. And I knew that the Lord was beckoning me. Would I take the step in faith and leave the dock that was my old life and step into that boat, whose destination I did not know?

I know very clearly that God gave me the grace at that moment to realize that the boat was going to a new life and that it would bring salvation if I just had faith to get in it and follow along the way the Lord was going to take me. Ever since then, there have been times in my life when the Lord has asked me to forge ahead in faith. As long as I have kept my eyes on the Lord's blessings and the Lord's power that emanates from his cross, I have been able to say "yes" to his invitation to follow him and to go along the path, to know his healing power to change my life.

DEEPER LEVELS OF CONVERSION

The message of the Lord to Leo on the day when he was baptized in the Spirit was clear. It was a call to leave the old life, to allow the cross to put to death all the passions that hold us to this earth in an unruly, disordered, and violent way. This further grace built upon and deepened the grace of conversion, making Leo even more aware of the Lord, his love, his authority, and his power to save. We see the beginning of that knowledge of God which

Paul describes in Galatians 4:6 and Romans 8:15, when he tells us that the work of the Holy Spirit is to create within our hearts a divine affection for God the Father. Thus, responding to the revelation of God the Father to our consciousness, we can freely say to him "Abba," Father.

It is instructive to reflect on the point in Leo's life when he stepped off the dock onto the boat—to see in our own lives if there has been a comparable moment. Many Christians, even after a dramatic conversion experience, find themselves discouraged and beset with habit patterns of sin and see no way out. But there is a way out. The turning point was named by Leo as being "baptized in the Holy Spirit." By whatever name this grace is called, a Christian must—through the action of the Holy Spirit—come to a conscious and living awareness of the reality and majesty of Jesus Christ and experience his power to change human lives.

This grace of revelation forms the basis of a consciously mature and commited Christian life. It makes the difference between a life of good intentions and mildly successful Christian virtue and one based on a clear awareness in faith of what it means to live in the power of the cross of Christ. This doesn't mean a Christian is perfect at this point of "faith" awareness. But it does mean there is a qualitative difference in his or her whole perspective and awareness of the reality that underlies the call to be a Christian.

You can recognize this work of grace because it grows within us. From that first moment when we become aware of God's presence and action, we arrive at a "living faith" knowledge of Jesus Christ as Lord and Son of God. The power to accomplish this is in the grace itself, if we agree to its working in our lives.

When this grace works its way in us, we *know* it. We have, in faith, the testimony of the Holy Spirit concerning the reality, the majesty, the mercy, and the power of Jesus Christ—most especially as he changes our lives by touching our hearts and moving us to give our lives to him. As this becomes habitual, we are aware that the Holy Spirit dwells within us.

One area of my life where I have really seen the power of the cross applied to deliver me from a bondage to real, deep-seated, lifelong hurt and mistrust is in my attitude towards authority. Because of the harsh environment that surrounded my relationship with my father, I came to have a deep-seated mistrust of authority and an anger and a resentment toward authority exercised in my life. I know that when the Lord brought me into Christian community, it was a great blessing. But one of the areas that had to be dealt with was my deep-seated mistrust of authority. The Lord poured out the grace for me to realize that I had to come to see God-given authority and its structure as being placed in my life for my protection, for my pastoring. It was God's love for me.

I know that I have had to repeatedly call upon the power of the cross of Christ to deliver me from bondage to the habit and thought patterns that had become so deeply engrained within me. Over a period of several years, I constantly called upon the cross every time old thought patterns, anger, resentment, or mistrust would come up into my mind or in situations where my actions had to change and come into submission and authority to God's will for my life. Over a period of time, the power of Christ's cross—when I would call upon it, believe in it, and act upon it—did change me. It did transform my inner attitudes from one of deep mistrust to a real trust.

A NEW WAY OF LIFE IN THE SPIRIT

We can learn from this description of Leo's interior struggle the true meaning of Christian asceticism. Leo is not describing a whole lot of acts of willpower by which he overcame disordered drives, bad memories, and deceptions concerning the role of authority in his life. No, he is speaking about a faithful calling upon the power of the cross of Jesus Christ—that act of love in which the Son of God died—to come and work a perceptible change in his life.

One of the greatest healings took place very recently. I was under a particularly heavy attack from a spirit of evil, and I could feel within myself the drive toward isolation, fear, anger, and suspicion that had at one time dominated my life. It was an important moment in the life of our community and in the life of my family as well. And I recognized that I was being assailed. I went to one of my brothers. In prayer, by the power of the Holy Spirit, the work of the spirit of evil was undone in my life. I know that it left me.

It was very much like my first conversion experience fourteen years ago. I was aware at that very moment that the evil spirit had left me. I knew then that I had been freed. I was aware of a newfound freedom. God acted in my life *in a way that completed the work of the last fourteen years, undoing the work of the first twenty-one and enabling me to have authority over my own life. By the blood of Jesus Christ, my life has been taken away from Satan and given back to me. The Lord has entrusted my life to me. Because of his Holy Spirit who dwells within me, I know that I can have authority over my life.*

Now in a new way, my desire to preach the gospel has gotten deeper. I look forward to sharing with others and serving them, bearing witness to the great work of our Lord Jesus Christ in my life. I can understand in some small way now what I never understood before in the lives of the great saints. St. Paul, for instance, wrote to the Philippians that he wanted his whole life to be poured out as a drink offering over the sacrifice of their faith (Phil 2:17). I now understand that.

I can see in my own heart a love and a compassion for those who are without the knowledge of the Lord—who are oppressed and held in bondage by poverty, by drugs, by anger, by violence, by ignorance. I know that my prayer has changed. I pray very little now for my own healing and very much for the world. I look forward to the day when I can give more and more of my time and my energy to glorifying the Lord, to worshiping him, and thanking him for what he has done for me and for the whole world. I want to preach the gospel in word, in example, and in compassion and service to all those to whom he will send me.

In this last dimension of Leo's life, we see how the work of darkness, which had woven together deep wounds and patterns of sin so many years ago, was finally undone in and through a long period of the healing grace of our Lord Jesus Christ. This work of the Holy Spirit brought Leo to the point where he could confide his own life and the care of it to the Lord Jesus. Thus, he was freed to set about the real work of life: caring for his family, the community in which he lives, and for all men and women wherever they are and in whatever need they find themselves.

In this book, I want to share with you the ways in which the Holy Spirit, the Life-changer, can change your life. The witness of Leo and the story of Bartimaeus can be your story as well. St. Augustine once said, "God made us without our consent but he will not save us without our consent."

The Lord has called us to a renewed, ongoing conversion to him. The Holy Spirit wants to make real in each of our lives all of the truths that we now hold by faith. He can be the most helpful counselor we've ever consulted—if we will only let him in. In fact, he can change our lives forever—if we will only let him. Call upon God and ask the Holy Spirit to show you how real he is. Let's pray:

> Come Holy Spirit, and show forth your radiant light. Come, Father of the poor, Giver of gifts. (Sequence for *The Pentecost Mass*)

Let's honestly admit our own powerlessness and poverty before the Lord. We have nothing to hide from God. He is the one who made each of us: he knows us intimately. By the power of the cross and the work of the Holy Spirit, we have been joined to God for all eternity.

Our days are numbered. They are weighed out, and we weigh out those days in keeping with the will of God. "So teach us to number our days that we may get a heart of wisdom" (Ps 90:12 RSV). We can invest each day the way the Lord God desires. We *don't* have all the time in the world.

Don't we want all our days to be filled most of all with rich personal relationships? Our need for intimacy and security is as real as our need for food and drink. We long to be truly loved and accepted just as we are. Many people seek this intimacy through a marriage relationship, yet the joining together of two weak and sinful human beings usually falls far short of satisfying these deepest longings. Where can we find such an intimate friendship? This is the issue chapter one explores where we learn of the wonderful and intimate friendship St. Augustine developed with God.

ONE

A Friend in Heaven

I LOVE YOU, LORD, not doubtingly, but with absolute certainty. Your Word beat upon my heart until I fell in love with you, and now the universe and everything in it tells me to love you, and tells the same thing to us all, so that we are without excuse.

And what do I love when I love you? Not physical beauty, or the grandeur of our existence in time, or the radiance of light that pleases the eye, or the sweet melody of old familiar songs, or the fragrance of flowers and ointments and spices, or the taste of manna or honey, or the arms we like to use to clasp each other. None of these do I love when I love my God.

Yet there is a kind of light, and a kind of melody, and a kind of fragrance, and a kind of food, and a kind of embracing, when I love my God. They are the kind of light and sound and odor and food and love that affect the senses of my inner man.

There is another dimension of life in which my soul reflects a light that space itself cannot contain. It hears melodies that never fade with time. It inhales lovely scents that are not blown away by the wind. It eats without diminishing or consuming the supply. It never gets separated from the embrace of God and never gets tired of it. That is what I love when I love my God. (*Love Song: Augustine's Confessions for Modern Man,* translated by Sherwood Eliot Wirt, Harper and Row, 1971, p. 124)

What brought St. Augustine to such raptures of love? He speaks of God with such intimacy and certainty. Yet this same man spent his entire youth pursuing sensual pleasures and illicit relationships, blown about by the ever-changing winds of his impulses.

Born in North Africa of a pagan father and a devout Christian mother, Augustine was brought up as a Christian. But the call of the world soon lured him to abandon his faith and live an immoral life. His sins steadily multiplied, even while he wrestled with God who wooed him as a lover.

Every time Augustine wanted to respond to God's offer of friendship, he confesses, "I was held back by trifling nonsense— old loves that plucked softly at my robe of flesh and murmured, 'Are you going to send us away? From this moment, forever and ever? It means you will never be allowed to do this and that again'" (*ibid.*, p. 116).

Pride, confusion, and lustful passion kept their hold on Augustine until he was thirty-three. His struggle finally dissolved in a stream of tears let loose under a fig tree in the garden of a friend in Milan. In the midst of this bitter dejection of spirit, Augustine heard a child's voice singing over and over, "Take up and read, take up and read."

He quickly reached for the Scriptures and read the first passage he saw: "not in reveling and drunkenness, not in debauchery and licentiousness, not in quarreling and jealousy. But put on the Lord Jesus Christ, and make no provision for the flesh, to gratify its desires" (Rom 13:13-14 RSV).

The fog of doubt immediately disappeared, replaced by a light of certainty in his heart. Thus St. Augustine's fiery passions became directed toward loving God and understanding the depths of his mercy.

Another very special friendship began in a quite different way when Abraham received an extraordinary promise from the Lord:

> Yahweh said to Abram: "Go from your land, from your family, from the house of your father, to a land that I will show you. And I will make of you a great people, I will bless you, I will make your name great, it will be a blessing. I will bless those who bless you; and those who curse you, I will curse; and in you will all the families of the earth be blessed." (Gn 12:1-3)

What did Abraham do to deserve such a promise? We are not told why God lavished such love upon this particular man. Actually, the call and the promise were unsolicited. We tend to think that friendship with God begins when we decide to take God as our friend. We usually commit ourselves to "be good" and promise God to do whatever he asks of us. We hardly ever do this unless we're in desperate need of help. But, of course, we are soon unable to keep such a hasty promise.

Friendship with God begins with God, not with us. "When we were still sinners, Christ died for us" (Rom 5:8). God chose Abraham to be his friend. God initiated the friendship and promised abundant blessing.

But friendship with God is demanding. Abraham needed to be obedient to what God said to him. It would not have been easy in those days to leave one's country and clan, and set out for a strange land with only God for a guide. Yet Abraham surrendered himself totally into God's hands and demonstrated his faith by obedience. Scripture says simply, "So Abram went as the Lord had told him" (Gn 12:4).

Abraham's relationship with God was secure. In calling Abraham into friendship, God seemed especially to desire a relationship which was deeply personal. He left room for Abraham to respond, express his emotions and fears, and raise his concerns.

The years of friendship between God and Abraham were many. Perhaps there were long periods of time when Abraham didn't hear from the Lord, or when he experienced doubt or confusion. But we do know that God was faithful year in and year out. God and Abraham were friends for life.

But what does this special friendship have to do with us? "If you are of Christ, then you are the seed of Abraham, heirs according to the promise" (Gal 3:29). In Christ, we become the children of Abraham, his spiritual heirs.

God loves us and wants each one of us to be his friend. From all eternity, he has wanted us as his own special people. The deepest motive of this divine will is the Father's wish to share his very own life with us in intimate friendship.

But what is our instinctive response to God's offer of friendship? We draw back and say, "But I'll lose control of my life. What will God ask of me? What hardships or suffering will he ask me to endure if I give him free reign? What if I can't do what God asks of me?" The heart of sin is that we do not trust God as a friend.

SIN IS A TERMINAL DISEASE

Suppose a man suffers troublesome headaches and a nagging tightness at the back of his neck. His doctor is unable to determine the reason for these symptoms and tries to reassure him: "It's probably too much stress. Try to relax more. Otherwise, you seem to be fine. I thoroughly approve of the way you've been taking care of yourself. You look great!"

Wouldn't the man suffering pain say, "Look, it's not approval that I need—it's healing. Most of me may look great, but these headaches are driving me crazy! If you can heal me, then heal me. If you can't, I'll have to find a doctor who can."

He then tries months of treatment by a chiropractor, but to no avail. When the man's symptoms become severe, his doctor puts him in the hospital for extensive testing. A malignant tumor is discovered—wrapped around the top of the patient's spinal cord. Surgery is impossible, and even repeated chemotherapy fails. Cancer soon claims his life.

In reality, we are all suffering from a terminal disease: the cancer of sin rages within all of us. "For the wages of sin is death" (Rom 6:23 RSV). Even a little bit of sin leads to death, just like a little bit of cancer left unchecked can kill us. But, unlike cancer, there is a cure. We can receive an eternal life from God.

If the best we can do for a friend lost in sin is to say, "You're really a good person," what has happened to the good news? If the best we can offer is encouragement or approval, where is the power of the cross to heal? Being a "nice person" is worthless in hell.

Sin is an awful mystery. We have all these different words for *sin*: *disobedience, rebellion, trespass, transgression, missing the mark.* It is very difficult to grasp exactly what it is we actually do when we sin.

Sin is not just a mistake, some sort of cosmic error. *Sin is a personal rebellion against God.* When we choose to do things *our* way rather than to obey God, we sin against his very personal love for us. We break our friendship with him.

In the beginning, humankind enjoyed a close friendship with God. The garden of Eden was a place of refreshment and peace where God provided for all of their needs. Adam and Eve loved to walk and talk with God in the cool of the evening. They were not embarrassed in their nakedness, either before God or one another: their communication was guileless; their hearts, open and pure. Adam and Eve personally knew God as the one who had formed them and breathed life into them. Our first parents shared their most intimate thoughts with God every day, as trusted friends.

But an enemy lurked within the garden, someone who hated this friendship and wanted to destroy it. The horrible reality of sin is clearly reflected in Satan's temptation of Eve, when the Serpent subtly introduced an element of doubt into her mind (Gn 3:1-7): "So, then, God has said: 'You shall not eat of any tree in the garden?'" Perhaps she had not heard God correctly.

Eve answered, "We may eat of the fruit of the trees of the garden; but God said, 'You shall not eat of the fruit of the tree which is in the midst of the garden, neither shall you touch it, lest you die'" (Gn 3:2-3 RSV).

Having found a listening ear, the Serpent then boldly contradicted God: "You will not die. For God knows that when you eat of it your eyes will be opened, and you will be like God, knowing good and evil" (Gn 3:4-5 RSV). Eve had the most trustworthy friend in the world and she chose to listen to the Serpent! He convinced Eve to take a closer look at God's motives. Perhaps greater satisfaction was available if she took matters into her own hands.

She was promised the knowledge of good and evil. The power to do what she wanted and then to be able, herself, to declare whether it was good or evil: "Then the woman saw that the tree was good for food, that it was attractive to the eyes and enticing to make one wise. So she took of its fruit and she ate, then she also gave it to her husband at her side, and he ate" (Gn 3:6).

When Adam and Eve reached out to grasp the knowledge of good and evil, they committed a terrible injustice against God. The injustice to God was not only that we sinned—but much more in the nature of our sin: we refused God's offer of a magnificent life of friendship. Our first parents completely mistrusted God and desired instead to have their existence under their own control. They chose to depend on their own resources to provide fulfillment and satisfaction.

This lack of trust inevitably gives rise to a feeling of alienation and fear. When Adam and Eve heard the Lord walking in the garden after they had sinned, they instinctively hid themselves. Suddenly they felt naked, ashamed, vulnerable, guilty (Gn 3:7). The intimate fellowship they enjoyed with God had been lost. Imagine their regret and sorrow!

St. Augustine also experienced this sense of deep loss and longing. Although God had begun to reveal himself to Augustine, he was unable to enjoy God. He laments,

> Your beauty ravished me, but I was soon snatched away again by the sheer weight of the world and its ways, to collapse dismally in its muck. Yet the memory of you remained with me, and I became convinced there was one to whom I ought to cleave, though I wasn't yet capable of doing it.
>
> I saw the invisible nature of God himself. However, I had not the strength to keep looking; in my weakness I recoiled and fell back into my old habits, taking with me nothing but a loving memory, as though I had sniffed the fragrance of eternity but was not able to eat of it. (*ibid.*, p. 98)

How often we choose, consciously or unconsciously, to remain in our sin rather than to turn toward God. Or to put it another way, we choose to do things our own way rather than trust God's love. We too are in bondage to sin because of our own fault, not only because of the sin at the dawn of history. By our own personal sins, we become *slaves of darkness*.

WE NEED A SAVIOR

How is it possible to recover once again that deep friendship with God which was lost when Adam and Eve listened to the lies of the Serpent? How can we be freed from the sins we have committed—indeed from the very drive toward sin which results in separation from God?

If God were to come to us revealed in all of his holiness while we were still in sin, his holiness would repulse us and drive us out. This is what the Bible means by "the wrath of God." His *wrath* is the absolute incompatibility between God's holiness and sin. God is not mad; God was never mad; God will never be mad. He is the one who loves us and took the initiative to save us.

Consider how a business solves problems. If a mortgage company runs out of stationery, the secretary orders more. If the copy machine breaks down, the office manager makes sure that it gets repaired. But if the number of mortgage applications takes a sudden nosedive, the president of the company would have to find a solution—or else the whole business would quickly go under.

The dilemma into which the human race had fallen required the attention of God himself. Our situation was desperately serious. God sent his only Son because he recognized the enormity of our problem. On the basis of our own resources, we would find it impossible to bridge the tremendous gulf created by the sin of our first parents.

Jesus poured out his life on the cross to restore our friendship with God, and to bring us into the covenant relationship that God established with Abraham. His blood repaired the injustice done to God by humankind's refusal of his gift of love. God provided his own Son as the perfect Lamb of sacrifice. The Son of God, the only man who ever lived who owed God nothing, died for our sins.

We cannot be holy and blameless in God's sight except in the blood of Jesus Christ (see Ephesians 1:7). When we receive this truth in faith, God reckons our believing as righteousness.

The truth of the gospel is that God can set us free from the cancer of sin. Our freedom consists in being forgiven our sins. This is what the death of Jesus Christ means. God has proven faithful to us as a friend.

Our *redemption*, therefore, is our *liberation from slavery*. In the Greek of Paul's day, the words which are related to this root mean paying a certain price to someone or symbolically to a god, in order to liberate a slave or a prisoner. When the blood of Christ is applied to our lives, we are bought back from the bondage of sin to belong to God.

We were bought at a great price. It cost the Son of God his blood to win us back to be a people for God alone. That is our worth. Each one of us is worth the blood of the Son of God—not by our own estimation, but by God's (see 1 Peter 1:18-19).

The obedience of Jesus in his death on the cross gave to God something far more precious than what was lost by our rebellion. Having become one with us, Jesus returned God's offer of love by accepting every detail of the Father's plan for his life and death. This plan drew out from his human heart the most perfect act of love possible. "Greater love has no man than this, that a man lay down his life for his friends" (Jn 15:13 RSV).

Augustine knew what it meant to be the friend of God, to be secure in his Son Jesus. He spoke of this work of grace and freedom in terms of being set on a guarded highway, rather than struggling through enemy territory:

> It is one thing to climb above timber line to the summit and catch a view of the land of peace, then to fail to find a trail leading to it, and so have to struggle through uncharted country, waylaid and beset by fugitives and deserters.
>
> It is quite another to move steadily down a posted highway to it, convoyed by the security troops of the King of heaven, unmolested by deserters who avoid the road like the plague. (*ibid.*, p. 103)

But how often we still feel so alone, surrounded by enemies and struggling to find a trail. When we feel the need for a faithful guide on this difficult journey, we can call on the Holy Spirit. Jesus has promised that his Spirit would be with us always. In Jesus, we are set on a secure highway that leads to the land of peace.

Do we know Jesus Christ? Do we know he died for us? Is that truth a fire and a lamp burning in your heart? Jesus Christ died for me. Jesus Christ died for you. Why? Jesus tells us, "Because I love you. I want you to be with me now and forever."

Listen to the witness of the Holy Spirit that the blood of Jesus Christ has cleansed us of sin and rebellion. This knowledge provides the only firm foundation for our lives. The blood of Jesus Christ speaks more eloquently than that of Abel (Heb 12:24). The blood of Jesus wins God's favor and enables us to enter into God's presence.

This touch of the Holy Spirit finally begins to give us a broken heart. Our rebellion—our resistance to God's love—begins to melt. As we penetrate the depths of his heart, we understand how desperately we need Jesus' death and all that has come to us through the love of Christ.

HOW TO BE FREE FROM CONDEMNATION

When we hear of our sinfulness, when we hear of how trapped we are in darkness, we become frightened. We say, "I can't make it." And we are right. We can't. But that's the *I* that has to go. Many of us suffer from a terrible self-image. That is not humility, but a work of the flesh, because we spend all day trying to hide it.

Augustine spoke of his own struggle with sin and condemnation as he tried to respond to God's call:

> When I vacillated about my decision to serve the Lord my God, it was I who willed and I who willed not, and nobody else. I was fighting against myself. As the Apostle would say, "It was no longer I that was doing it, but sin which dwells within me." Such was the penalty of a sin committed in conditions of greater freedom by Adam, whose son I am.
>
> And such was my psychological condition. I kept condemning myself bitterly while twisting and turning in my chains, trying to break them, because it was a very small matter that still held me. . . . My introspection plumbed the secret depths and brought together all my misery in plain sight of my heart. (*ibid.*, pp. 115-116)

Do you see the huge difference between introspection and self-awareness? Introspection is the work of the flesh: we keep thinking about ourselves and how sinful we are. But a humble awareness of our desperate need for God is the fruit of revelation. We resist this revelation because we are proud and fearful of submitting to God.

The same Apostle Paul also spoke of the freedom and friendship God offers to his chosen people: "If God is for us, who is against us? Who shall bring any charge against God's elect?" (Rom 8:31, 33 RSV). God, the Father? He is the one who is justifying us. Jesus Christ? He died for us. More than that, he rose for us and now sits at the right hand of God interceding for us.

How can we have a bad self-image when God the Father made us, God the Son redeemed us, and God the Holy Spirit dwells within us? If God is not going to condemn us, then what is our problem?

Our problem is a spirit of condemnation. This particular accuser of the brethren deeply afflicts everyone. We open the door to this spirit by our sin and by our pride—by not accepting the witness of the Holy Spirit.

"There is therefore now no condemnation for those who are in Christ Jesus" (Rom 8:1 RSV). The *now* means since the time of the resurrection. Because we belong to Christ and are cleansed in his blood, we can enter into the presence of God's holiness:

> By this we shall know that we are of the truth, and reassure our hearts before him whenever our hearts condemn us; for God is greater than our hearts, and he knows everything. Beloved, if our hearts do not condemn us, we have confidence before God.
> (1 Jn 3:19-21 RSV)

The word used here for *confidence* is *parresia*, which in Greek suggests two images. It first evokes the notion of a free and confident discussion between friends. Real friends don't carefully weigh every word they say, but speak their mind freely and openly. The other image is of local residents standing up in their own town council, where they can boldly speak their opinions.

The essence of freedom in a relationship is lack of coercion or constraint. God made us; he knows our humanity. Jesus came to earth as one of us; he knows our weakness. God does not expect robot-like obedience. God will not override our free will—that part of us that reflects the image of God.

The point is not to be *good*—but to be *God's*. God desires confident, abiding friendship with each of us. Ask yourself, "Do I have that kind of friendship and freedom with God?" It would be a rare person who could say yes, and yet don't we all deeply long for that very reality?

What is the obstacle? We don't accept the testimony of the Holy Spirit that witnesses to the power of the blood of Jesus Christ to set us free from sin and condemnation. When we are in sin, we're blocked to the witness of the Spirit.

The biggest obstacle is our pride that wants righteousness on our own terms. We want *our* understanding, *our* grasp of salvation, to be the basis of our freedom. Rather than *receive* freedom, we want to think it out and control it. When we are not free before God, what do we do? Are we quick to examine *our* personalities, *our* thought patterns, *our* sins, *our* repentance? These may be helpful to consider at some point. But we should first look to the witness of the Spirit who will impress upon us the truth that Jesus Christ has washed us in his blood. Only when we take our stand *in Jesus*, washed in the blood of Christ, can we know freedom from the bondage of sin and condemnation.

Take some time in silence to kneel down and pray.

"Lord, my mind is a wreck. I'm full of turmoil, darkness, and sin. But I'm opening myself at this moment to submit to your truth. I want to accept the witness of your Spirit, because I want to know this freedom of heart.

"If I am under guilt or a spirit of condemnation, have mercy on me. I want to have a free heart before you. I know I can't earn it by my own righteousness, or because of what a great person I am, or even because of how hard I'm trying to repent.

"I can be free before you only because of the power of the blood of Christ to purify me, to heal me, to bring me to repentance, to bring me to heaven. Only in Christ can I be free. Please, send your Spirit to convince me of that reality."

Augustine, too, cried out to the Lord in such a way, and God sent his Holy Spirit to convince him of the saving power of Jesus Christ. Finally, he was able to abandon himself utterly to God's mercy and love:

I came to love you late, O Beauty so ancient and so new; I came to love you late. You were within me and I was outside, where I rushed about wildly searching for you like some monster loose in your beautiful world. You were with me but I was not with you.

You called me, you shouted to me, you broke past my

deafness. You bathed me in your light, you wrapped me in your splendor, you sent my blindness reeling. (*ibid.*, p. 125)

God will hear *your* cry and answer you as well. It may take time to work through the obstacles in your life, but God will show you how to walk in greater freedom, step by step.

We can look forward to the fulfillment of the redemption of God's people in life everlasting. We possess the hope of heaven—a deep and abiding friendship with God. By the power of the Holy Spirit, we are able to walk in that friendship even now.

But how can we acquire the kind of faith that Abraham possessed? That seems crucial to entering into friendship with God. Do we just try harder to believe? Faith seems necessary to know God, but first we have to know God to receive faith. What is our part and what is God's part? What is faith, anyway?

TWO

Faith Comes Gift-Wrapped

M IKE WAS DRIVING TO WORK EARLY THAT MORNING, his blue mini-van humming along on the expressway as usual. This was actually a fairly pleasant drive—not too much traffic, very few trucks trying to pass him, lots of beautiful countryside.

Daily commuting was tiring, but at least provided time for praying and thinking, and for being thankful for such a good life. Mike had everything a man could want—a beautiful wife, two wonderful children, lots of Christian brothers and sisters, a good job, a new home.

Mike was in the prime of his life, the very model of a joyful man who loved God and faithfully carried out his responsibilities. He was especially gifted at sharing the good news of his faith with his co-workers. In fact, the weekly Bible study that Mike had organized at work was meeting at noon that day.

But God paid an unexpected visit that morning. Mike's car suddenly careened across the median—almost striking a truck whose driver somehow managed to veer out of the way. Mike was killed instantly when his car flipped over. His family and friends were left to pick up the fragments of shattered dreams.

No one ever knew what caused the accident. Mike had been very tired lately from his heavy work schedule. Had he fallen asleep at the wheel? Did he have a sudden heart attack? Whatever the cause, the funeral was a time of joy—for Mike's sake. Everyone knew Mike was prepared to meet the Lord.

Have you ever thought about what it will be like when you die? Most of us have, in our more sober moments. We hope death will claim us quickly, so we won't have to face its slow and agonizing approach. Is anyone ever really ready to die, or to deal with the loss of a loved one?

Death is one of the few common realities we all face. Yet we spend our lives fearful of the prospect. In my work as a priest, I often minister to dying people and their families. I have seen hundreds of nervous and embarrassed friends and relatives come to the bedside of a man who is dying and say something like, "Cheer up, Harry. You're looking better. Chin up. See you this afternoon." They know, and Harry knows, that he is dying. Yet they are unable to face it. Death is an awful problem without a solution—unless we know the reality of the Lord and the power of his resurrection.

Even for Christians, death is unknown, shrouded in mystery. Those who have already died cannot come back to tell us about it. Even if they could, it would be like explaining the sensation of skydiving to someone who has never done it. We can never quite know the feeling until we have made the jump ourselves. And we instinctively cling to solid ground, the tangibility of what we know.

The life of faith is something like that. *When we believe, we begin to die because we have loosened our grasp on our lives and on our minds.* We begin to stand less on what we can see, and to take God's word for what is true.

Believing God is never easy: the call to believe is always a call to risk. God wants to be our friend. But we need to step out in faith and really trust him. Believing God is like jumping off that cliff and *knowing* we will land safely—because God himself has promised to carry us.

How are we able to take such a leap—the leap of faith?

The Holy Spirit gives us the power to yield to God, to believe, to accept the witness of God. In order to restore our fractured relationship with God, the Holy Spirit needs to bring us to faith in Jesus.

Even if our life looks pretty good, the truth is that—without Christ—we are in darkness, on our way to death. Yet if we accept the testimony of the Holy Spirit about the death and resurrection of Jesus Christ, God has an infinitely beautiful plan for our lives.

FAITH IS GOD'S WORK IN US

God is always bearing witness to the truth of who he is and what he has done for us in his Son, Jesus Christ. We have to hear the good news and accept it. "Faith comes from what is heard, and what is heard comes by the preaching of Christ" (Rom 10:17 RSV).

To believe is to accept this testimony and say, "That's it. I'm going to base my life on that. If you say Jesus can save me and bring me safely home, I believe you."

Faith is not merely accepting that God's plan of salvation is a very good idea and being loyal to that idea. People say "I believe in God" and by that they mean they accept God's existence. James says the devils do that and they tremble (Jas 2:19). Evidently, they know who God is and what power he holds more clearly than most of us.

Faith is not an intellectual opinion which we hold because it is logical and reasonable. "Atheists hold that there is no God, but I happen to believe that there is. Some people don't think that Jesus Christ is the Son of God, or that his death and resurrection can save us from eternal death, but I'm persuaded that they are wrong."

That is opinion. You cannot build your life on that. Faith rests on the certainty of God who has revealed himself in Jesus Christ. Faith *resembles* opinion in the sense that we do not have total evidence for what we believe, but it *differs* in that we have complete assurance that what we base our lives on is true.

Faith is a way of knowing. We know, not because of our own intelligence or resources, but because of the light of God and the power of God at work in our minds. The Holy Spirit brings us to that knowledge. We cannot go to the library and learn it through research. Such knowledge is not under our control. We have it only because God is continually giving it to us in the anointing of the Holy Spirit. But it is real knowledge—the specifically Christian way of knowing.

Faith is knowing God, committing our lives to God and basing our lives on what he says. Faith flows from a personal relationship of love: we trust what the beloved tells us. We learn to place more confidence in spiritual realities than in what our senses or emotions tell us.

God has said, "I love you. I have sent my Son to die for you. If you accept the cleansing power of his blood, you will be free for all eternity. This is what I offer you." We say, "God, I thank you. I commit my life to you. I love you. I accept this salvation."

Faith is a work of God in us to which we agree. Sometimes we get that far, and we think we understand, "Ah, yes . . . it is faith." The problem is that we then try to make faith another work. So it becomes this work of faith. We think, "I have to muster up more faith"—as though faith were that human work by which we are made right with God.

People are not saved by an experience of salvation; they are saved by the work of God in Jesus Christ. Faith is a gift of God by which we are set free from the bondage of sin. "For by grace you have been saved through faith; and this is not your own doing, it is the gift of God—not because of works, lest any man should boast" (Eph 2:8-9 RSV).

Then what is our part? To agree to what God is accomplishing within us. Faith is a gift which God holds out to us. He wraps this wonderful present for each of us individually. Will we accept or refuse this gift?

Though God offers it freely to us, the personal cost is enormous: dying to ourselves, our ways, our plans, our dreams, our values. In order to receive this gift from God, we must first loosen our grasp on whatever already fills our hearts and minds.

The Spirit makes the truth attractive to us by an *exterior* revelation that has its own power to draw men and women to Jesus. But there is also an *interior* touch of the Holy Spirit, impelling us to believe. We are always free, but the Holy Spirit loves us so much that he is not above pushing us to believe. The Spirit urges us, "Believe, will you? Listen, will you? Surrender, will you? Your life depends on it!"

In this way the Father draws many to the Son—by the touch of a divine operation, moving the hearts of men and women to believe. God wants to give us eyes of faith to see that Jesus is the best friend we'll ever have.

SEEING JESUS

God had a problem. How could he reveal himself to humanity? How could we come to know who he is, what he is like, how much he loves us? Prophets and angels served as messengers, but the words they spoke were often ignored.

There is a story about a little boy who was having trouble getting to sleep one night. He had a bad dream and was afraid of the dark. His father came to reassure him. "You're not really alone. God is here with you," said the father—hoping that fact would provide some added comfort. "I know that," the son replied. "But sometimes I need somebody with skin on."

Jesus, the only Son of God, came to earth as one of us—so that we could *see* God as one of ourselves. When we see Jesus, we see the Father. "No one has ever seen God; the only Son, who is in the bosom of the Father, he has made him known" (Jn 1:18 RSV).

At the Last Supper, Jesus said to his disciples, "I am the way, and the truth, and the life; no one comes to the Father, but by me. If you had known me, you would have known my Father also; henceforth you know him and have seen him" (Jn 14:6-7 RSV).

Philip still did not grasp what Jesus was saying and said, "Show us the Father, and we shall be satisfied." Jesus said to him, "Have I been with you so long, and yet you do not know me, Philip? He who has seen me has seen the Father; how can you say, 'Show us the Father'? Do you not believe that I am in the Father and the Father in me?" (Jn 14:8-10 RSV).

Seeing spiritual realities requires eyes of faith. We are like extremely near-sighted people whose eyes can focus only on objects close to them. Others with far-sighted vision assure us that beautiful panoramas can be seen. So we visit the optometrist to be fitted with lenses especially suited to our own eyes. When we first put on our new glasses, we are astounded at the clarity and beauty beyond our natural vision. Faith is like a new pair of glasses.

Those who knew Jesus as the son of a carpenter were very near-sighted. They saw only a man—special in many ways, but an ordinary man. It takes revelation to open our eyes to see who Jesus really is.

The role of John the Baptist was to prepare the hearts of the people by preaching repentance. He was such a powerful figure that the Jews began to wonder if *he* was the Christ. God had told John how to recognize the Christ. He was Jesus' cousin, yet even John did not know who Jesus was until it was revealed to him.

After Jesus came to him to be baptized, John said,

> "I saw the Spirit descend as a dove from heaven, and it remained on him. *I myself did not know him;* but he who sent me to baptize with water said to me, 'He on whom you see the Spirit descend and remain, this is he who baptizes with the Holy Spirit.' And *I have seen and have borne witness that this is the Son of God.*" (Jn 1:32-34 RSV)

All through the Gospel of John, there is the promise that the believer will *see* Jesus, that is, see him as he really is. When John speaks about *seeing* Jesus, he means a revelation of the Holy Spirit to the spirit of the believer showing who Jesus Christ really is. This grace is what we mean today when we speak of being baptized in the Holy Spirit.

We are promised such an awareness that it can be called sight, even though it is not sight as we commonly understand it. Indeed, it requires renouncing the desire to see with our own eyes or to see on our own terms. "Now faith is the assurance of things hoped for, the conviction of things not seen" (Heb 11:1 RSV).

Seeing spiritual realities can be compared to someone looking through a microscope for the first time. This person thinks that the tangible objects surrounding us form the substance of reality. Yet a high-powered microscope suddenly reveals a whole new world of atoms and molecules in constant motion. We are enabled to see microscopic life that surrounds us all the time, yet previously we were unable to perceive it. A completely new reality is revealed.

The Holy Spirit provides power to see spiritual realities. Thus, we know Jesus Christ, love him, and believe in him—even though we do not see in the sense that our minds are satisfied. "Though you have not seen him, you love him; even now, though you do not see him, you believe in him and rejoice with an inexpressible and glorious joy, for you are gaining the goal of your faith, the salvation of your souls" (1 Pt 1:8-9).

We do not need to have emotional experiences in order to see Jesus. We do not need to reach great intellectual heights, yet we can see Jesus. Simeon, a devout Jew who lived in Jerusalem, was looking for the coming of the Messiah:

> And it had been revealed to him by the Holy Spirit that he should not see death before he had seen the Lord's Christ. And inspired by the Spirit he came into the temple; and when the parents brought in the child Jesus, to do for him according to the custom of the law, he took him up in his arms and blessed God. (Lk 2:26-28 RSV)

Simeon was full of joy because he had seen Jesus. There was nothing special about this baby—no halo around his head, no angels carrying him, no blast of trumpets to announce his entrance into the temple. The Holy Spirit revealed to Simeon that this child was the Christ.

Jesus came to reveal God the Father to his people, Israel. They were expecting the Messiah, but many of them were looking for someone different. They did not see in Jesus a king, as the son of David, one who could lead them out of political captivity. They did not have eyes to see that their bondage went much deeper than lack of religious and political freedom.

Take Judas Iscariot, for example. It seems that Judas was zealously committed to the cause of Jewish freedom. He saw in Jesus the kind of leader who could inspire the people and rally them against the Romans. He was expecting a political messiah, but Jesus failed to use any political strategies to stir up the people.

Finally, Judas became fed up and agreed to betray Jesus for thirty pieces of silver. Judas could not change his mind and seek to understand Jesus for who he really is. Later when he saw that Jesus was condemned to death on the cross, Judas was filled with regret. He returned the money to the Pharisees and hanged himself in despair. This last act of self-preoccupation graphically demonstrates his true condition: spiritually blind and in bondage, under the dominion of Satan, unable to receive from Jesus what Jesus alone could give him.

Jesus came among the people of Israel to bring the good news of release from captivity:

> And he came to Nazareth, where he had been brought up; and he went to the synagogue, as his custom was, on the sabbath day. And he stood up to read; and there was given to him the book of the prophet Isaiah. He opened the book and found the place where it was written,
>
> "The Spirit of the Lord is upon me, because he
> has anointed me to preach good news to the poor.
> He has sent me to proclaim release to the captives
> and recovering of sight to the blind, to set at
> liberty those who are oppressed, to proclaim the
> acceptable year of the Lord."
>
> And he closed the book, and gave it back to the attendant, and sat down; and the eyes of all in the synagogue were fixed on him. And he began to say to them, "Today this scripture has been fulfilled in your hearing." And all spoke well of him, and wondered at the gracious words which proceeded out of his mouth. (Lk 4:16-22 RSV)

Yet these same people rejected him soon afterward. They did not have eyes of faith to see Jesus as the Christ. They asked, "Is not this Joseph's son?" Filled with wrath at his claim, the crowd tried to throw Jesus over a cliff (Lk 4:29).

Those who believe in Jesus have eyes of faith because the Spirit has been given to them. They can now see Jesus Christ as the Son of God. It is the work of the Spirit that each of us can gaze upon him whom our sins have pierced and have our own minds pierced to understand what happened on the cross.

We receive life from that gaze when we understand who he is and why he was crucified. We begin to catch a glimmer of his majesty with God the Father, bearing the glorified wounds that he received in order to save us. Let us pray for the eyes of faith truly to see Jesus.

FALLING IN LOVE WITH JESUS

Loving Jesus cannot be reduced to sentimental feelings. To love Jesus is to want to be with him, to want to serve him, to be grateful for salvation, to know what he has done for us, to want to be his disciple. The author of First Peter states, "Though you have not seen him, you love him; even now, though you do not see him, you believe in him and rejoice with an inexpressible and glorious joy, for you are gaining the goal of your faith, the salvation of your souls" (1 Pt 1:8-9).

What a remarkable statement! He is not offering words of empty comfort. That will not help when life gets tough. The people to whom he was writing were experiencing serious trials and persecutions. People can be psyched up to contribute to a building fund, but they cannot be convinced to live under daily pain and suffering by saying, "Cheer up! Tomorrow will be better." That will not cut it.

Either we know Jesus Christ and love him, or we're not going to make it. If we don't know and love Jesus, there is nothing big enough or real enough in our lives to stop us from caving in to the constant pressures of the world.

Although we never saw Jesus, we know him and love him. Through prayer, we talk to him, and he talks to us. Isn't that remarkable? Doesn't that reality prove that we have new life—a life that is not bound by time and space, or by the flesh, our own mind, or human resources?

This new capacity is the work of the Holy Spirit. It does not mean repeating by memory, "It says here that if I love him, I will keep his commandments. I'll keep his commandments, and therefore I love him." That is not what these words mean.

But don't many of us approach our Christian lives in this way? We try to keep the rules from a feeling of obligation. We start in the Spirit and end in the flesh. If we're going to keep all God's commandments by ourselves, we'll need a lot of willpower. That type of behavior merely means that we are good legalists, and Jesus had the sharpest rebukes for the Pharisees who functioned on this level.

Faith makes us righteous. We do not become righteous because of the way we live. Compliance with the law does not necessarily mean that we love Jesus. God looks at the disposition of our hearts, not just our actions.

We cannot treat God impersonally. "The one who has my commandments and keeps them is the one who loves me. That one will be loved by my Father and I will love him and I will manifest myself to him" (Jn 14:21). The Lord is saying, "If you let me touch your heart and bring you into real knowledge of me, then you will be established in love and empowered to demonstrate that love by faithfulness to my commandments."

The keys to faith are trust and obedience. When we believe in God and love him, we trust him as our closest friend. We put our lives into his hands. He is more precious to us than anything else. When there are difficult decisions to make, we turn to him for counsel.

This is what the New Testament means when it says that *we walk by faith and not by sight* (2 Cor 5:7). It does not mean that we do not know anything or that our minds are a blank. We can't keep saying, "Yes sir, yes sir," to all this—and then keep trying morally, on our own willpower, to put this life into action. We will simply get more and more discouraged that way because it simply does not work. That is not the Christian life.

Jesus did not die and rise again so that we could be discouraged. He died and rose so that we would have a new life—a life of intimate friendship with God who loves us.

FAITH TO LIVE BY

In the truest sense of the word, Jesus and the Father enjoyed a deep, abiding friendship. Jesus never moved a muscle unless it was the will of his Father. All of his energy, all of his inspiration, all of his resources, all of his motivation came from his Father. "Truly, truly, I say to you, the Son can do nothing of his own accord, but only what he sees the Father doing; for whatever he does, that the Son does likewise" (Jn 5:19 RSV).

Consider the example of Jesus driving the money-changers out of the temple with a whip. Can you picture the scene? Sheep and oxen running helter-skelter, pigeons flying everywhere, tables overturned, coins scattered, angry people yelling. Jesus was filled with zeal for his Father's house (Jn 2:13-22).

On another occasion the disciples brought Jesus some food to eat. They knew he had not eaten for a while and would be hungry. Jesus refused and said, "I have food to eat of which you do not know" (Jn 4:32 RSV). His disciples wondered who else had brought him food. But Jesus was filled by ministering to the needs of people such as the Samaritan woman. "My food is that I do the will of the one who sent me, and that I bring his work to completion" (Jn 4:34).

The person who believes in Christ lives by faith. We say, "Jesus, you are the living Son of God. Be Lord of my life. Let me be crucified with you. I'm through trying to get what I need from this sinful world. Money, material possessions, power, success, approval—these things don't give me meaning or energy. My life comes from you alone."

When we say Christ died for us, we are already beginning to understand what it means that Christ lives in us. "I have been crucified with Christ. I am living, but not really I: Christ lives in me. The life I now live in the flesh, I live in faith, faith in the Son of God, who loved me and gave himself up for me" (Gal 2:19-20).

That ego of which I am conscious—that ego which forms the basis of my self-awareness—is dead. It's useless, a waste of time. That ego that I spent most of my life building up—scrap it! It's not worth anything. It will only kill me.

Just think about how self-centered we all are. There is very little that happens in a day that we don't judge in reference to ourselves. We always consider, "How will that affect me? What's in this for me? Will I get what I need in this situation?" There is practically a cult built around "looking out for *numero uno*."

But we were not created for that. We were created to love and worship God. The work of the cross brings about a shift in the basis of our lives. It is "I" who lives. But, the "I" who lives is the "I" transformed by Christ—not the ego that we've so carefully nurtured all our lives. That old self is dead.

"Christ in me" is only dimly perceived at times. Now our knowledge and faith are imperfect. We see but dimly the spiritual realities revealed by the Holy Spirit. But one day we shall understand fully and meet our Savior face to face. Then faith and hope will have realized their object and we will be enveloped in God's love. This hope of union with God forever urges us on in our journey of faith.

As the Holy Spirit helps us to receive this gift of faith, what will new life in Christ be like? What does it mean to be born again? Sometimes a gift has strings attached—like those "free vacation" offers we receive in the mail. Is more required of us than mere acceptance?

How can we expect the Spirit to be active in deepening our faith? Faith seems so intangible, so hard to grasp. What visible signs does God provide to help us to experience faith as a powerful reality in our daily lives?

THREE

A Brand New Life in the Holy Spirit

K NOWN AS THE WHITE HOUSE "Hatchet Man," Charles Colson had become one of President Nixon's closest confidants by the age of forty. But in the midst of tremendous power, Colson discovered his true powerlessness. He was entangled in the scandal of Watergate and charged with obstruction of justice. He pleaded "guilty" to the charge.

In the aftermath of Watergate, Jesus revealed himself to Chuck Colson. A business associate's statements and life of faith stuck in his memory. During months of turmoil, he especially envied the kindness, sincerity, and peace radiated by this man. So Colson made an appointment to talk with him again, and was surprised to hear Jesus described as a personal friend rather than as an historical figure.

Colson found himself stubbornly objecting within his own mind. *A life of faith couldn't be that simple in the complex world of politics,* he thought. Yet as the conversation continued, his internal resistance began to melt. When he said good night and sat down in his car, Colson suddenly dissolved into a flood of tears.

Pride stopped him from going back into his friend's house, but Colson did cry out to God for help. This plea from a softened man began a search for spiritual truth. The once powerful political figure was forced to face his own pride and selfishness, but found that God's mercy was even greater. All his previous "astute" objections now seemed foolish. Chuck Colson was born again into the kingdom of God when he humbly surrendered his life to Christ.

God worked dramatically during Colson's long months in a federal prison. His definition of power completely changed. A new man with a new kind of influence sprang forth from the ashes of his political career. Colson founded Prison Fellowship in 1976, just three years after resigning as Special Counsel to the President. Since then his life has been devoted to helping others know the powerful love of God.

Jesus speaks about being born into the kingdom of God in a very interesting encounter recorded in the third chapter of John. Nicodemus was a Pharisee, a ruler of the Jews, probably a member of the power establishment of his day just as Charles Colson was. Evidently, he had been observing Jesus and was impressed with his words and deeds. He wanted to pursue his concerns personally to find out who Jesus really was.

Concerned about his reputation, Nicodemus came to Jesus at night. "Rabbi, we know that you are a teacher come from God; for no one can do these signs that you do, unless God is with him" (Jn 3:2 RSV). Nicodemus already had eyes of faith. Most of the Pharisees did not think that Jesus came from God.

Jesus answered him:

> "Truly, truly, I say to you, unless one is *born anew*, he cannot see the kingdom of God." Nicodemus said to him, "How can a man be born when he is old? Can he enter a second time into his mother's womb and be born?" (Jn 3:3-4 RSV)

Nicodemus was puzzled by Jesus' answer. This concept of being born again was difficult to fathom. He was already a mature man; a fresh start seemed impossible. A grown person certainly cannot climb back into the womb to be born anew. Yet Jesus said that we could not enter the kingdom of God unless we receive it like a child (Mk 10:15).

Jesus explained:

> "Truly, truly, I say to you, unless one is born of water and the Spirit, he cannot enter the kingdom of God. That which is born

of the flesh is flesh, and that which is born of the Spirit is spirit. Do not marvel that I said to you, 'You must be born anew.' The wind blows where it wills, and you hear the sound of it, but you do not know whence it comes or whither it goes; so it is with every one who is born of the Spirit." (Jn 3:5-8 RSV)

The same Greek word means both *wind* and *spirit*. Jesus likened the Spirit of God to the free and invisible wind. We can hear it and see the effects of its passing, but we don't know where it comes from or where it goes. The new life of which Jesus was speaking comes to birth by the power of the Spirit of God, not of flesh.

Nicodemus was still unable to understand what Jesus was talking about. "How can this be?" he asked.

Jesus answered him:

"Are you a teacher of Israel, and yet you do not understand this? Truly, truly, I say to you, we speak of what we know, and bear witness to what we have seen; but you do not receive our testimony. If I have told you earthly things and you do not believe, how can you believe if I tell you heavenly things? No one has ascended into heaven but he who descended from heaven, the Son of man. And as Moses lifted up the serpent in the wilderness, so must the Son of man be lifted up, that whoever believes in him may have eternal life." (Jn 3:10-15 RSV)

Jesus came to die on the cross that we might be born again to eternal life, that we might enter into the kingdom of heaven. We enter into that new life by faith. What does it mean to be born again?

BORN AGAIN

"Blessed be the God and Father of our Lord Jesus Christ who, in keeping with the greatness of his mercy, has given us a new birth unto a living hope through the resurrection of Jesus Christ from the dead" (1 Pt 1:3).

The essence of rebirth is captured by this statement. By rising from the dead, Jesus broke the power of sin and death for himself and for us. *By faith,* we are born anew to this living hope, this hope of victory and eternal life. We are born into the family of God, for "Every one who believes that Jesus is the Christ is a child of God" (1 Jn 5:1 RSV).

Rebirth in Christ does not merely enable us to behave better. Just living a moral life is not the final goal. When we are born again, we have a whole new life, a new energy, a new power within us. Coming to know God as our Father—as the very source of our life—empowers us to live a *spiritual life* which transcends the limitations of our own resources.

The Christian faith offers us a way to reestablish our relationship with God—a way to be *born again.* In First Peter 1:23 (RSV) we read: "You have been born anew, not of perishable seed but of imperishable, through the living and abiding word of God." The *Word* is God's eternal truth, embodied in his Son Jesus Christ. This Word of God contains all of his wisdom and creative power. By this Word we are reborn.

This new life is given to us by the Holy Spirit. The only way we can describe this truth is to say, "It's like being born all over again." It makes no difference how old we are or what our past has been like. "If any one is in Christ, he is a new creation; the old has passed away, behold, the new has come" (2 Cor 5:17 RSV).

New life in Christ reveals a new way of understanding the world. The reality that we face is no different than that which everyone else faces. We just know how to understand it, because of the work of the Lord in our minds. The Word of God reveals to us the reason our lives are ruled by fear and disorder. God offers wisdom and power that set us free from the difficulties that hold the human race in bondage.

People should be able to look at us and say, "There is something different about you. Why aren't you anxious and fearful? The world we live in is enough to frighten anyone! Why aren't you controlled by anger and greed like everybody else I know?" And we can tell them about the work of the Holy Spirit in our lives.

That is the good news. We can say to someone, "You can live a different way, you know. You don't have to be filled with fear and anxiety. I know it's true because I was dead and now I'm alive. I was brought from darkness to light, by Jesus Christ pouring out his Holy Spirit. None of this happened because I especially deserved it or because I have such strong willpower. It came about through the mercy of God. If he can do it for me, he can do it for you." That is what it means to be born again—to have a whole new life by the power of the Holy Spirit.

BORN OF WATER

How does this miracle of new life happen? The fundamental birth or rebirth of a Christian is through faith—through hearing the Word of God and accepting it—as did Chuck Colson. This birth is completed and perfected by the sacrament of baptism. Baptism has always been called "the sacrament of faith."

We need eyes of faith to see the spiritual reality behind the sacramental signs: the action of the Holy Spirit bringing believers to birth. Through the water of baptism, God puts the old self to death and brings forth a new person.

Paul compared baptism with being buried with Christ:

> Or are you unaware that we who were baptized into Christ Jesus were baptized into his death? So then, we were buried with him through baptism into death, so that just as Christ was raised from the dead through the glory of the Father, so, too we might walk in newness of life. (Rom 6:3-4)

This sacramental ritual in which Christ acts in and through his body, the church, embodies a monumental fact: we are joined to God because we are united with Christ in his death. Baptism plunges us into Jesus precisely in his sacrificial act of love. Through the water of baptism, we are healed of the sickness of sin. God cleanses us, washes away our sins—even the stain of original sin inherited from Adam and Eve.

Baptism is normally the first step in accepting God's salvation. As Catholics, we are usually baptized as infants because of the faith of our parents. Then we are nourished by our family and the church to help us grow in faith. The Eucharist celebrates our coming of age when we enter fully into the worship of Christ in the Mass and receive his body and blood. Confirmation is the sacrament by which we receive the gift of the Holy Spirit in greater measure to empower us to live a fervent and mature Christian life, entering more fully into the mission of the church as adults.

This lifelong process is essentially a *deepening* of faith, whereby faith becomes knowledge, while still remaining faith. Faith is always a response to revelation. Our faith deepens as that revelation becomes more personal. The tragic fact is, however, that many people have received all the sacraments of initiation and yet do not know the Lord personally and do not experience his power in their lives.

In the fourth-century church of Jerusalem, candidates for baptism prepared intensively throughout the forty days of Lent—three hours a day, under the instruction of their bishop. To be eligible for the Lenten preparation, the catechumens had first to complete three years of preliminary instruction. Their preparation for baptism was interior, with the stress on teaching the mind. They wanted to be ready for that moment of rebirth so they could experience its full power.

Since they regarded water baptism as having real power, they expected God to act. This is the way baptism should be seen. Through baptism, the Word of God is rendered alive, active, and dynamic—not in some abstract way, but in a living, powerful way by the action of the Holy Spirit.

Through eyes of faith, these early Christians saw the new birth of baptism as a literal reality. They did not approach it out of some sort of loyalty, and then later say, "Well, the New Testament says it, the church teaches it, so somehow, I must have been born again and have new life." They did not experience that kind of mental shuffle.

Coming into the *fullness* of baptism is a life-changing process undertaken by God within us to which we say "yes." The whole process can be described as one of faith. The role of our will in this is not to produce results but to agree to the work of God within us. Faith is the soul of the whole process, the work of God within us by which we submit to and embrace the reality of Jesus' cross and resurrection.

This process is like a spiritual open-heart surgery. God brings about a profound spiritual change in us that literally gives us a new lease on life. But he won't operate without our consent. We can distinguish three aspects of this life-giving process: (1) *information*, or knowing the truths of the faith and yielding one's heart to them; (2) *commitment*, a decision by which someone commits his or her whole life to Jesus Christ; and (3) *faith experience* and *knowledge*, which come by the action of God through the sacrament of baptism.

We need both to know and experience the truth, to hear and understand the good news. The truth of God's saving work needs to take firm root in our minds and hearts, by the power of the Holy Spirit. Yet we will not understand the truth of our salvation unless we decide we really want it. The gospel requires such a decision, a personal commitment to God: "I believe it; I will stake my life on it." Here we need to ask ourselves some hard questions:

Do I believe that I really need saving? Am I ready to renounce the illusion, deceit, and rebellion that characterize life without God? Do I believe that God's judgment on reality is right and that mine is wrong?

Am I ready to stop trying to be the center of the universe? Am I ready to commit myself to Jesus as my Lord, as the Son of God, and as the personal master of my life?

Once we have surrendered our lives to Christ, the Holy Spirit provides a faith experience. God puts his seal on the faith that is already there. We experience this *seal* as a revelation in our spirit that Jesus Christ is the Son of God. We *know* this is true. The martyrs of the Christian faith were prepared to give up everything else—including their lives—for the sake of this knowledge.

"In him you as well, having heard the word of truth, the good news of your salvation, having believed, were sealed with the Holy Spirit of the promise" (Eph 1:13). First, we heard the truth. Second, we made a decision to accept the good news. Third, our faith was sealed with the Holy Spirit. *Baptism is the seal of God upon the faith given to us by the Holy Spirit.*

St. Cyprian provides an excellent example of the full reality of baptism. A lawyer in Carthage who had been on the fringes of Christianity for a while, he finally decided to be baptized at the age of thirty-six. The following excerpts are from a letter which Cyprian wrote to a friend concerning what happened to him. (The translation is given in the book *From Darkness to Light* by Ann Field, Servant Books, 1978, pp.189-190.)

"Until that time I was still living in the dark, knowing nothing of my true life. I was completely involved in the world's affairs, influenced by all its changing moods and troubles, and exiled from the light of truth. I had indeed been told that God offered men and women a second birth by which we could be saved, but I very much doubted that I could change the kind of life I was then living. Frankly, I could not see how a person could cast off his fallen nature and be changed in heart and soul, while he still lived in the same body as before. How is it possible, I asked myself, to change the habits of a lifetime instantaneously? How can one suddenly rid oneself of accumulated guilt and break with sin that has become so deeply rooted in one's life?

"... These were my thoughts. My past life was burdened with so many sins that I saw no way ever to be rid of, that I had grown accustomed to giving way to my weakness. I despaired of ever being any better. Consequently I simply humored my evil inclinations and made no attempt to combat them.

"But at last I made up my mind to ask for baptism. I went down into those life-giving waters, and all the stains of my past were washed away. I committed my life to the Lord; he cleansed my heart and filled me with his Holy Spirit. I was born again, a new man.

"Then in a most marvelous way, all my doubts cleared up. I could now see what had been hidden from me before. I found I could do things that had previously been impossible. I saw that as long as I had been living according to my lower nature, I was at the mercy of sin and my course was set for death; but that by living according to my new birth in the Holy Spirit I had already begun to share God's eternal life."

St. Cyprian heard the truth of the gospel and decided to accept it. By repenting of his sins, he personally experienced a radical conversion to Jesus Christ. All of Cyprian's doubts disappeared in this new birth of baptism.

BORN OF THE SPIRIT

Water baptism and the receiving of the Holy Spirit are meant to be inseparable. We enter into the life of Christ through faith and the sacrament of water baptism. In water baptism, we are sealed with the Holy Spirit, who comes to dwell in our hearts:

> He saved us, not because of deeds done by us in righteousness, but in virtue of his own mercy, by the washing of regeneration [baptism] and renewal in the Holy Spirit, which he poured out upon us richly through Jesus Christ our Savior. (Ti 3:5-6)

The Holy Spirit does not reveal anything different from what has been confided to the church for all ages. Yet the gift of being renewed by baptism in the Holy Spirit, which is the term often used in the charismatic renewal, enables us to understand this truth in a new way. We grasp what it really means that Jesus Christ died for each one of us. In our day God is renewing his people precisely by restoring to them the three key elements of the baptismal process: information (hearing the gospel), decision (repenting from sin and accepting Jesus as Lord), and a genuine experience of faith (a new way of knowing Jesus, personally, as Lord).

Baptism in the Holy Spirit is a common way in the church today of describing a personal, abiding experience of the reality and presence of Jesus Christ, manifested in a transformed life and the use of spiritual gifts. This powerful experience of God's love is meant to bring us to a deeper awareness. Little by little, we let God change our minds through repenting of our sin and learning the truths in Scripture. From this process comes an ever deepening conversion, and knowledge of the reality and majesty of Jesus, the risen Son of God.

It is not an uncommon experience in our time that the first awareness of the grace of baptism in the Holy Spirit is accompanied by deep joy, an emotional sense of fulfillment, and the manifestation of gifts, such as tongues, prophecy, and healing. This has been the mystery of God's way with us in the twentieth century. By this perceptible action, God begins a process that is meant to bring us to a personal knowledge of Jesus Christ and an experience of the power of his cross to free us from sin and the habit patterns of sin.

We should all pray for a further outpouring of the Holy Spirit in our lives, by whatever name we call this grace. Even though the Spirit already dwells in us by baptism, we must become aware of his action and direction if we are to live our Christian lives as adults. We should ask the Holy Spirit to fill us to overflowing, to bring us to a personal encounter with God in his Son Jesus Christ.

Since being baptized in the Spirit is such a personal experience, perhaps it would be helpful to hear the story of a college student who was brought face to face with God in this way. The student, Catherine, experienced a frustrating inability to overcome sin in her life, even though she was a baptized Christian. After several years of constant struggle and guilt, she finally told God, "I've really tried to live as a Christian, but I'm just worn out and defeated. I'm going to go it on my own for a while."

That proved to be the most painful year of Catherine's life. Her relationships became a nightmare; she quickly gained thirty pounds as her addiction to food worsened; old patterns of sin like petty theft threatened to land her in serious trouble. Finally a new boyfriend helped to restore some stability to Catherine's life. But after several months, he became frustrated with her emptiness and ended the relationship.

Catherine was brought to a screeching halt. With no one left to cling to for life and support, she walked the snow-covered campus crying out to God to rescue her. She had always resisted a total surrender of her life to God because of existing relationships or plans to pursue. What if God had other ideas? But now Catherine had nothing left. She begged God to take her life in his hands, whatever the consequences.

Catherine heard about a local prayer meeting and tried to find out when and where the prayer group met. That Sunday, she read someone's testimony in the church bulletin about "finding the love of Christ through the love of other people." It sounded like Greek to Catherine. Desperation led her to call this complete stranger to ask the meaning of this puzzling phrase. Her conversation did not yield any clearer understanding, but a sense of peace began to ease her heavy heart. This seemingly foolish step toward God was at least some sign of her sincerity. Catherine hoped God would meet her the rest of the way.

Just five days after her first cry to God for help, this utterly sad young woman slipped into the back row of that week's prayer meeting, hoping no one would notice her. Soon after the small group began to sing in tongues, she suddenly experienced an overwhelming awareness of God's presence. God seemed to be tangibly surrounding Catherine and telling her of his personal and intimate love for her.

A flood of peaceful tears welled up from the deepest part of her and seemed to wash away years of pain and loneliness. For the first time in her life, Catherine was able to praise God and tell him that she loved him. Catherine had always *known about God* and believed in him, but now she *knew* God personally as an intimate friend, faithful and trustworthy in every way. She was able to surrender her deepest desires into his loving hands.

Catherine had been baptized in the Holy Spirit. Her life would never be the same. The Word of God in Scripture now brings new life to her. The transforming power of the resurrection has become alive in her by the work of the Holy Spirit.

JESUS IS THE BAPTIZER

"Baptism in the Holy Spirit" is an action of the risen Savior. The Holy Spirit reveals to the spirit of the believer the true reality, majesty, and saving power of the Son of God. We are enabled to surrender our lives in a deeper way to God's saving work. We are empowered by the Holy Spirit to die to sin and live to God.

Over the next several months after Catherine's personal encounter with God, her faith became a river of living water flowing out of her heart. She couldn't read enough of Scripture. Prayer seemed natural and spontaneous. The sacraments became rich with meaning as Catherine experienced the real presence of Christ. Patterns of sin like greed and lust no longer held power over her. The power of the Holy Spirit had come to dwell inside of Catherine to transform her heart and mind.

The action of the Holy Spirit was obvious in many new ways. Catherine experienced a new and deep love for her brothers and sisters in Christ so that she was able to reach out to them and offer support. Her mind became hungry to learn more about this new life of faith. She received Scripture passages from the Lord that spoke directly to difficulties she faced. The gift of tongues offered a new way of praising God in the Holy Spirit.

Before the Son of God became man, before he died and rose again, the human race was unable to receive the indwelling work of the Holy Spirit in this life-changing way. The Spirit was obviously at work from the very beginning in God's work with his people. But there is a new presence now. One of the most famous texts in this regard is John 7:37-39:

> "If anyone thirsts let him come to me; and let him drink whoever believes in me. As the Scripture says: 'Rivers will flow from him of living water.'" Now he said this concerning the Spirit which those who believed in him were going to receive. For the spirit was not yet, because Jesus was not yet glorified.

This passage is speaking of faith. When we experience a thirst in our spirits that water cannot quench, Jesus says to believe in him, to come to him—and he will satisfy that thirst. Jesus knows that all of us are thirsty for the Holy Spirit, the living water.

Jesus was addressing those who were able to admit this spiritual thirst. A lot of us know we're dry, but we have our own ways of temporarily satisfying that thirst. Catherine tried to satisfy her spiritual emptiness by seeking out new relationships or by overeating. Jesus was inviting people to come to him to not only have this thirst quenched, but also to be filled to overflowing with streams of living water.

What Scripture is Jesus referring to when he says, "Out of his midst shall flow rivers of living water"? It is actually a combination of Scriptures. John means that Jesus himself is the source of this river of living water. The Holy Spirit comes from Jesus. If you wish further information, you could read my book, *Baptism in the Holy Spirit: A Scriptural Foundation* (Steubenville, Ohio: Franciscan University Press, 1986) for an exposition of these and other Scriptures.

Jesus is the baptizer in the Holy Spirit. We can receive the fulfillment of what Jesus promised when he said that out of his own midst would flow rivers of living water. On the cross, from his opened heart, there flowed the blood of salvation and the water of the Holy Spirit (Jn 19:34).

There would be no baptism in the Holy Spirit if the Lord had not undergone the baptism of death. Jesus took the cup of God's wrath and drank it down. We enjoy the fruit of the cross. Because Jesus died for our sins, believers are able to be baptized by Jesus in the Holy Spirit.

Being baptized in the Holy Spirit is not a delightful experience to console us for a moment—but rather a deepening of the new life which Christ lives in us. Indeed, it can be painful at times as the Spirit reveals sin and deceit in our hearts. The Spirit gives power to the Word of God. "For the word of God is living and active, sharper than any two-edged sword, piercing to the division of soul and spirit, of joints and marrow, and discerning the thoughts and intentions of the heart" (Heb 4:12 RSV).

Catherine's initial experience was an overwhelming sense of joy, yet she still had to deal with her sin. For instance, the Lord showed her that her flirtatious behavior was unbecoming to a Christian woman and although it was difficult at first, she also learned to let go of frustration when something didn't go the way she had planned. Catherine discovered that God was working all things out for good if she would only obey him. She learned to hear the Lord and respond to the promptings of his Spirit.

The Spirit of God lives in us and becomes the very principle of activity within us—moving us from the depth of our own will so that we love God with our whole heart and mind and strength. That is exciting! The Holy Spirit is trying to change our minds—to break us out of captivity.

Ironically, those who live in our modern, Western culture are often victims of the most profound captivity. Although we enjoy material abundance, we can suffer deep spiritual poverty and hunger when we are blind to the deeper spiritual reality of God. When we are bound in such spiritual captivity, we are like a race of solitary cave dwellers who live in total darkness.

We have heard that God exists. In fact, we may believe this and once in a while speak to this God. Occasionally something even happens in our solitary caves so that we know by inference, "I guess God must have acted." But each person is alone inside his or her cave—closed off from any meaningful interaction with God or with others.

In a strange twist of irony, our captivity stems from what is called the Age of Enlightenment. Its cardinal principle is that God does not act in this universe. Whatever happens is explainable in terms of the energy, resources, and causality available to the universe.

When people accept this false view of reality, they suffer a spiritual regression of sorts. Cut off from God in their minds and spirits, the captives return to their darkened caves, spiritually speaking.

Through coming to know the Lord Jesus personally, we are freed from our solitary existence as cave dwellers. Now we can come out into the light of day and recognize God's saving action in our lives. The Holy Spirit is poured out into our lives to deepen our relationship with God. We don't have to know the Son of God by inference any more, but we can know the anointing of the Holy Spirit. We say, "It really was you, wasn't it? You really are the Son of God, aren't you?"

Even if you are not involved in the charismatic renewal and the terminology of the renewal is alien to you, decide now to seek personal conversion and renewal in the Holy Spirit. After all, the fullness of the Holy Spirit is available to all baptized and confirmed believers—seek him out.

We are all called to know the Lord and his power personally in our lives. The outpouring of the Spirit brings our faith to completion precisely by making the revelation of Jesus personal and life-changing. This power is given to enable us to eliminate sin in our lives and witness to the truth of Jesus to others.

But sin in our lives doesn't disappear overnight. How does the Holy Spirit accomplish this cleansing process? We experience our weakness every day. It often seems impossible to live up to the expectations of God. How do we apply the power of the cross to our own lives? How can we experience freedom from the bondage of sin day in and day out?

FOUR

Our Battle
Against the Flesh

I T WAS A BITTER COLD WINTER'S DAY in rural Ontario, Canada, as I worked in the woods, felling trees for firewood. The wind cut through me like a sharp knife. My movements became labored as I trudged through the thick snow.

My mind drifted back to a time in early summer when I had been in that same place in the woods. It had been a clear, sunny, dry day with the wind rustling through the leaves. The squirrels and chipmunks had scampered about, chattering noisily and foraging for food. Not far away, several deer had grazed in contentment.

Yet now I was struggling in weather well below zero—the landscape stark and bereft of life, the sun giving off little warmth. I sighed and reminded myself that by early afternoon it would be dusk and the cold would become unbearable.

What a difference the change in seasons had made in my experience of being in the woods, I reflected. The summer day had given me delight, while I did not consider the winter day pleasing at all. Yet in the rhythm of nature, both summer and winter are necessary.

Our life with God reflects the same realities: the beautiful moments contrast with the difficult awakenings and the unpleasant intrusions. Appreciating God's beauty is easy when it doesn't cost us anything. But when we invite Jesus to become

Lord and live in our homes—even in our very hearts—life becomes challenging. It begins to cost us.

There is the rub. We human beings are most likely to appreciate God's work when it's convenient, when we don't have to die to ourselves. But God wants to come and live *within* us—not just on a pleasant summer's day in the woods. And the Spirit of God speaks to us many times when it's not convenient.

What is it in us that says "be quiet" when we're disturbed, or "go away" when we're annoyed? Paul calls it *the flesh*: an internal drive toward self-preservation and self-glorification, that bondage to sin in every one of us that causes us to resist the Lord and shut out others.

Without the transforming power of the cross, our thoughts and deeds are driven by the flesh. When we are baptized in the Holy Spirit, we receive new life in Christ and are empowered to follow him. But being born again does not end the battle. Our transformation in Christ is a lifelong process—a rocky road full of obstacles, including our stubborn flesh.

If we do not know how to deal with this bondage to sin, what happens? *We go on doing good works out of our own energy and hope that no one will realize how terrible we really are.* We think, "Everybody else seems to be doing well, but I have this battle raging within me. I experience anger, lust, jealousy, revenge. I'm held captive by fear and anxiety. What's wrong with me? How can I call myself a Christian?"

The flesh is opposed to our spirit—that dimension of the human personality which is open and available to be enlivened by God. We are created in the "image of God" (Gn 1:26) by virtue of our spirit, created precisely for the purpose of worship and submission to God. God breathed the "breath of life" into us so that we could transcend the mere physical life of the animal world (Gn 2:7).

But the *flesh* has more to do with our *self-will* than with our physical bodies. Dying to self is ultimately done in the will, and requires an ongoing decision of the heart and mind.

The reality of death to self is stark. Now we have to die. When the Spirit of God comes to dwell in us, we begin to experience a real battle. That is one of the signs of the indwelling Spirit. Dead people do not experience pain. Dead people have no struggles.

Baptism and personal renewal in Christ do not yield instant

victory over our stubborn flesh. Why do we continue to experience this bondage to sin?

THE CHAINS OF SIN

St. Augustine provides a graphic description of the battle that can rage within us because of the flesh:

> The enemy had taken hold of my will; he had clamped a chain on it and shackled it. For my will had been perverted and had manufactured lust; the more I gave in to lust, the more it developed into a habit, and when I failed to check the habit it became a necessity. These were all links in the chain that held me enslaved. The new will that had begun in me—and made me want to be free to worship and to enjoy you, God, the only certain joy—was not yet strong enough to overpower the old will that had become tough with age. So there were now two wills battling it out inside me, one old, one new; one carnal, one spiritual; and in the conflict they ripped my soul to pieces. (*Love Song: Augustine's Confessions for Modern Man*, translated by Sherwood Eliot Wirt, Harper Row, 1971, p. 108)

What is the reason for this universal bondage to sin? Ancient Sumerian and Akkadian myths attempted to explain our predicament in terms of a mistake. When their gods became drunk one night, they made little clay people. But because the gods were not in complete control of their wits, the results were less than perfect. Each person ended up with some sort of deformity: one with a broken arm, one with a broken leg, one with a misshapen head, and so on.

The "modern" explanations seem just as far-fetched. Repeating this ancient solution, the famous French existentialist Jean-Paul Sartre, said in effect: "You can't figure it out. Life is just absurd, it has no meaning. The evil, the injustice, the pain, the confusion in life are just there. Human beings are bent on their own destruction and there is not much you can do about it."

Another contemporary opinion holds that the injustices of life are created because we are underdeveloped: intellectually, socially, psychologically, economically, politically. People who think this way assure us that as the human race progresses, the reality which the ancients called "sin" will gradually be eliminated.

The school of the Enlightenment held this view. The optimism of the nineteenth century participated in it. We see it in the view that all humankind is aspiring somehow to be Western middle class consumers. Two world wars have begun to shake our confidence! The fact that we can now blow up the world at any time is another indication that something more serious is wrong with us.

But how easily we all fall into this trap! So often we try to rationalize our rebellion or cope with our sin. We think, if only we had a better paying job, we could buy a house and life would be so much easier. Or we think, if only we could read all these books, we would be healed of our addictions and compulsions.

Our condition is more grave than improved economics or politics or pop psychology or literacy or any other noble efforts can ever touch. We are in bondage to sin. The Word of God tells us the reason for this thrust towards sin. At the dawn of the human race, our first parents rebelled against God. They activated the power of sin. Sin is now a malevolent power which rules over human life because we personalize it and accept it into our lives, following the pattern set by our first parents.

We have to deal with this fact of sin. Any spirituality that does not take sin seriously is founded on an illusion. To say that men and women "really mean well" is simply not borne out by reality.

We are held in captivity because we do not know how to deal with this drive toward sin. The principle reason Christians do not grow in their life with God is that they do not treat sin realistically.

In fact, sin—as a power—takes on structural forms in our lives. These structures result from many individual sins, but they are given an overriding power independent of those sins by their collective and structural existence.

By structures of sin, I mean patterns of activity in our lives which govern situations in such a way that sin is advanced and virtue impeded. For example, think of a family where the husband has no real concern for his wife and children. Instead, he is consumed with the drive to make money and enjoy himself. He is unfaithful as a husband and a father, spending almost all his time either working or pursuing expensive leisure activities. The wife gets angry and retaliates by drinking and neglecting her children. In turn, the children rebel and do not learn to respect authority.

In such a situation, you can see the structure of sin. It exists almost independently of any member of the family, yet it dominates the entire household. It is composed of all the individual acts of sin, but exercises an influence that is independent of any one member of the household.

These sinful drives and the structures they create when left unchecked show up most clearly in our emotions and through our flesh. But the flesh is not primarily identified with sexual immorality. "Now the works of the flesh are plain: fornication, impurity, licentiousness, idolatry, sorcery, enmity, strife, jealousy, anger, selfishness, dissension, party spirit, envy, drunkenness, carousing, and the like" (Gal 5:19-21 RSV).

Look at how many of these works of the flesh have to do with human relationships creating structures of sin that exert influence over families and other groupings in society. The deepest, most characteristic expression of the flesh is *isolation* or *alienation*—to cut us off from God and from one another.

When the Bible speaks of "the flesh," it does not mean something we get rid of when we die. The *flesh* means a *state of alienation from God.* Apart from Christ, we are alienated from God, ruled by all those forces opposed to God—whether they be demonic, social, physical, universal, or political. To die while captive to the flesh means to die eternally.

The most characteristic expression of the Spirit is *communion,* communion with God and with one another. "But the fruit of the Spirit is love, joy, peace, patience, kindness, goodness, faithfulness, gentleness, self-control; against such there is no law. And those who belong to Christ Jesus have crucified the flesh with its passions and desires" (Gal 5:22-24 RSV).

Think now of the structures of grace and recall our earlier example of how a particular family demonstrated the structures of sin. By contrast, in this model, the husband and father cares for his family. He consciously decides to bring his children up to know the Lord. He is concerned about them and shares his faith with them, providing for his children both materially and spiritually. As a husband, he loves, respects, and is faithful to his wife. She responds, caring for the children and supporting all that he is trying to do for the family. The children, seeing this, respond positively to their parents, love them, and respect their authority.

This family lives in a structure of grace, just as surely as the first family inhabits a structure of sin. It is independent of any one person, yet it facilitates a whole life of grace.

Our fallen human condition, however, is opposed to the will of God. We need to fight a daily battle against the desires of the flesh and will experience that battle until we die. But the flesh, as our physical condition, is also the *hinge of salvation*, as Tertullian used to say. That is the way God gets at us. If we let him, the Lord can begin to destroy the structures of sin in our lives and begin to construct structures of grace, which will lead to a whole new way of living for us and those we love.

Consider the example of St. Augustine. Because he was enslaved by such overpowering appetites of the flesh, he knew that something was out of joint in his life. Intellectual zeal prompted him to seek answers in astrology, esoteric religion, and philosophy.

But Augustine continued to experience the dilemma Paul describes in Romans 7:

> But I see another law in my members warring against the law of my reason and making me captive to the law of Sin which is in my members. A wretched man am I! Who will deliver me from the body of this death? (Rom 7:23-24)

Augustine was especially held captive by his passionate sexual desires. In an effort to reform his life, he decided to take a wife and became engaged to a suitable young woman. Since the girl was under the legal age, the marriage had to be delayed. Meanwhile, Augustine struggled with his attachment to a prior mistress:

> The woman who shared my bed for so many years was torn from my side as an "impediment" to my forthcoming marriage; but my heart, broken and bleeding, still clung to her. She sailed back to Africa vowing she would never know another man, and leaving with me our natural son.
>
> I was impatient at the prospect of a two-year delay before I

could marry my intended wife, and being a slave to sex rather than a lover of marriage, I acquired another unattached female. This prolonged and renewed and aggravated the disease of my soul under the umbrella of well-established custom, and made certain that the habit would persist into the life of marriage itself. (*ibid.,* pp. 89-90)

St. Augustine experienced death in his body because of his bondage to sin. But God was at work in his mind and heart to show him the way to life:

Your right hand reached to the bottom of my heart and emptied out its dregs of death and corruption. All you asked was that I cease to want what I willed, and begin to want what you willed. . . . My mind was free at last from the corroding anxiety of running around trying to get somewhere, and continually scratching the itch of lust. (*Ibid.,* p. 119)

Surrender is the key! All we can do about the flesh is to turn it over to the Lord, so that he may crucify it through the power of the cross. *Freedom is accurately perceived as total surrender to God, rather than the unrestrained individualism desired by the world.*

When we surrender ourselves to the Lord, the Holy Spirit replaces the flesh as the governing principle in our lives. The structures of sin that had characterized relationships begin to disappear and are replaced by structures of grace. It's like being under new ownership. Let's say, for example, that the wealthy parents of a spoiled son give him a beautiful new Cadillac as a high school graduation present. Unfortunately, he's a reckless driver, and the car is soon covered with scrapes and dents from several accidents.

At this point, instead of correcting their son, the parents foolishly give him a new Corvette. They sell the damaged Cadillac to a car lover who restores it to mint condition. This new owner drives the restored Cadillac carefully and maintains it well—since for him, it is a prized possession.

We are like that Cadillac. Before we become God's possession, we are driven ruthlessly by the flesh, the world, and the devil. But when we come under new ownership by surrendering our lives to Christ, God lovingly restores us to full beauty, the life of grace. Moved along by the careful guidance of the Holy Spirit, we can avoid many scrapes and dents. We begin to experience a whole new way of living characterized by grace.

RULES WON'T SAVE YOU

The message of freedom is that the Holy Spirit replaces the flesh as the real source of power in us. That is why Paul says: "For freedom Christ freed us; stand firm then, and do not be encumbered again with a yoke of slavery" (Gal 5:1).

Paul was worried that the Galatians would put themselves back under the law—thinking that keeping all the rules would save them. That does not lead to salvation, but merely ends in slavery. It is the flesh trying to save the flesh.

Without realizing it, many Christians have been living under the law. God reveals himself to them and teaches them how to live. By applying their minds, they learn a lot about how to be good Christians—and then by their own willpower, try to put this into operation. Essentially, they are trying to save themselves by being good. But God wants a decision of the heart and will, not simply actions which spring from our unsubmitted resources.

Our striving to reach self-imposed norms so that we will be "safe" with God brings us only death. Why? Because this approach reflects a very impersonal way of relating to God, who loves us with the intimacy of a faithful friend. Consider how dead a marriage relationship would be if the husband and wife were only striving to obey certain rules of behavior, rather than warmly loving each other.

Those of us who were raised Catholic before Vatican II have often experienced this difficulty. We had a tendency to think that if we just followed the rules, we'd be saved—going to Sunday Mass, confession once a year, not eating meat on Fridays, and sending our children to Catholic schools.

These efforts may be somewhat successful, yet there is something inside that weakens Christians who are trying to keep all the rules. Those who rely on willpower alone inevitably experience a certain difficulty, a certain resistance from within.

This internal enemy is the flesh. We are freed from the hold of the flesh through the Holy Spirit who comes to dwell within us. By the power of the Holy Spirit, we can stop striving to be perfect on our own terms and instead begin to rely on the grace of God.

Surrendering to the Lord means opening ourselves to humility and love. We can't be worried about appearing foolish, or exposing our weaknesses and faults. Our desire for perfection merely reflects pride and fear—works of the flesh that drive us to protect and exalt ourselves.

Our weakness or inability to do good is part of our flesh. *But an even greater obstacle to God's grace in our lives is our fearful reaction when we fail to keep the law.* Anxiety and frustration operate in us to the degree that we have not in fact died to the law.

An example would help to illustrate this important point. After Joan sends her three young children off to school, she rushes off to a busy day at the real estate office where she works. She often feels overwhelmed by all of her responsibilities at home and on her job. Even though she earnestly prays and asks God to help her, the frustration only increases.

Joan's burden is so heavy because she is trying to do everything perfectly, please everyone and appear to be the perfect Christian. God knows her weaknesses, but she feels insecure in his presence because she isn't living up to her own expectations. In her busyness, she often neglects to spend time in prayer. She doesn't want to ask for help for fear of exposing her weaknesses. And so she keeps struggling in the flesh to fulfill her obligations, without receiving the power and wisdom from the Lord to do what is really necessary.

Paul states this truth in Romans: "For if you live according to the flesh, you are going to die; if however, by the Spirit, you put to death the activities of the body, you will live" (8:13). Paul is warning us that when we are angry, fearful, or frustrated because of our own self-centered striving to do good, we are still under the law.

We are called to die to the law in the same way that we died to sin. The law has been fulfilled in Jesus Christ, who came to set us free from the law of sin and death:

> For [regarding] the ineffectiveness of the law, in that it was weak because of the flesh, God, sending his own Son in the likeness of sinful flesh and "for sin," condemned Sin in the

flesh, so that the just requirement of the law might be fulfilled in us who walk not according to the flesh but according to the spirit. (Rom 8:3-4)

God condemned sin not only in the flesh of Jesus, but in all those who are joined to Jesus by the Holy Spirit. The flesh—our sinful nature—is condemned, robbed of its power. We need to put confidence in the grace of Christ to free us from sin and death. The Holy Spirit lives in us and wants to give us authority over our flesh.

But sometimes, even though the Spirit of God lives within us, we do not yield to his authority. Instead, we are overcome by pride, fear, greed, lust, or selfishness. Consider the example of a young woman who wants to be married. She has prayed about her desires and felt God reassure her that he would provide a good husband. But her patience begins to wear thin.

A good-looking guy at work begins to pay extra attention to her and then asks her out on a date. He seems to be really nice, but she doesn't know if he's a Christian. Her loneliness and longing for a relationship prompt her to go out with him. After all, she rationalizes, perhaps she could evangelize him.

One thing leads to another. Before she fully realizes what has happened, she falls in love and goes to bed with him. As it turns out, the guy is not at all interested in a serious relationship and soon jilts her. This young woman has been seriously damaged because of giving in to the desires of her flesh.

Or consider an even more insidious work of the flesh. A young man who has been a Christian for a while subtly begins to think of himself as better than others. He reasons, "I'm sure glad my life isn't a mess like Joe's. Why doesn't he get his act together?" Pride and self-righteousness begin to dampen this man's love and service to a friend who desperately needs God's mercy.

Believers who do not have authority over the drives of their flesh are immature to some extent, not ready to be used by the Lord in full power. Since they have not fully yielded themselves to the authority of the Holy Spirit, sins such as pride, fear, lust, anger, or greed can put a significant dent in their ability to love. Their witness to the love of Christ can be diminished by their own unrighteousness.

We can take this negatively or positively. Our response can be, "I'm never going to make it!" or "Isn't it fantastic that the Spirit of God is willing to give me grace to take authority over my unruly desires!"

REALIZING OUR DEATH TO SIN

The second stance is the truth: our realization that this is a promise. God is able to bring it about in our lives. When we surrender to the authority of the Holy Spirit, we are *dead with Christ*.

Now this is an ideal. But it is also a fact, a spiritual reality. To know that the work of Christ is going on in our lives means to experience that we're not quite as egotistical as we were last year. We're a little more God-centered and other-oriented. We're not quite as hung up on wearing an impressive wardrobe or driving a Mercedes. We're not quite as much in need of success or approval from our neighbors and co-workers.

Despite this good news, we say that we do not notice that we are dead to sin because we still commit those "little" nagging sins every day. There are two reasons for that: first, we have yet to personalize our death to sin to the same degree that this work of Christ is available to us; and, second, we have habit patterns of sin. We have inherited a whole way of personalizing this structure of sin which is now our own. There are habits of sin ingrained in our personality, like the weathered and eroded surface of a riverbed that runs downstream.

If someone, for instance, has a habit of alcohol abuse, he or she can be touched by the grace of Christ and be free from the dominance of that drive from the outside but still have to deal with the habit pattern from the inside. Or to use another example, imagine a child in a family dominated by structures of sin, suddenly moving into a family characterized by the structures of grace. The child has "died" to that first situation, but brings with him or her a whole set of instincts, reactions, and memories that needs to be set right by an ongoing death to the former way of life.

All of this is the work of the Holy Spirit. We do not will it. We *let* the Lord bring it about, because Christ lives in us and takes us to the foot of the cross.

THE SCANDAL AT THE HEART OF THINGS

The cross of Christ is a puzzle, a mystery, a scandal—and it is the source of all the life and hope we have as Christians. It is both very familiar and very remote. We pray before the cross; we wear it; we sing about it. But when we get close to the mystery, our flesh rebels.

"Let's not dwell on death and sacrifice and sin," we say. We try to evade the implications of the cross, to rationalize it, to make it a comfortable arrangement. "New life? Great!" our flesh says. "I've got it made. It's all done. No more struggle. I can just keep sinning. Jesus has already done everything for me."

Paul asks, "What then shall we say: Let us remain in Sin so that grace may abound?" He knows that our flesh would love to do exactly that. "Of course not. We who died to Sin, how can we still live in it?" (Rom 6:1-2).

The power to change comes from our new life in Jesus Christ. The Lord brings about the change. To follow Jesus, we must give up control over our lives. For example, we can't just set our hearts on getting married, having three children, and owning a large suburban home with two cars in the garage. If that dream fails to materialize, discontent can begin to undermine our relationship with God.

God needs to be in control of our lives. We cannot know in advance where it will all lead, what will be required of us, what the new man or woman will look like. It is a real death—a death to self. Only some are willing to pay the price.

A television commercial for a more expensive brand of oil filter warns, "You can pay me now . . . or you can pay me later." The meaning is clear. If we do not attend to the everyday maintenance of our car with quality products, the repair bill for a breakdown will be steeper down the road.

In the same way, if we do not take care to obey God every day—and pay the price in denying our flesh—then we will ultimately face a much stiffer penalty. The cost of discipleship is not cheap, but the rewards are eternal.

Are you willing to pay the price? Do you really want to change? We can know everything about our sin. We can see the fear, the pride, the self-concern. We can see the situations where we are always angry, resentful, lustful, or cowardly. We can know it's wrong.

Often, the Lord himself has to give us the desire to change. We have to beg him for the grace to want to live righteous and holy lives. If the Spirit of God dwells in us, we can pray every day, "Lord God, show me your love for me. Holy Spirit, reveal your presence to me. Change my heart."

The surest sign of the work of the Holy Spirit of God in us is the desire to do the will of God. That does not come from the flesh. Believe me, we do not mean well in our flesh! The desire to obey God comes from the work of the Holy Spirit in our lives.

"So if the Spirit of the One who raised Jesus from the dead dwells in you, he will also give life to your death-directed bodies because of his indwelling Spirit in you" (Rom 8:11). If the principle of the Spirit of life is within us, we begin to experience the depth of our sin. But we will also have a new desire to repent and be free of it, to put it to death in the power of the cross.

How can this death occur? We need to accept personal responsibility for our sin and personally decide to die to it. The Holy Spirit makes our decision active in us through the grace of baptism, when we are joined to Jesus in his death. We share Christ's resurrection life by joining in his death. This decision means dying to ourselves.

That is the central paradox of our Christian faith: we live by death. Listen to the words of Jesus:

> If any man would come after me, let him deny himself and take up his cross daily and follow me. For whoever would save his life will lose it; and whoever loses his life for my sake, he will save it. For what does it profit a man if he gains the whole world and loses or forfeits himself? (Lk 9:23-25 RSV)

Many of us were baptized as infants and received, to the measure of our capacity, the work of our Lord Jesus Christ. But this work must go on. We must inform our minds concerning the reality and authority of God, the true state of humankind, and the greatness of the work of Christ. The work must extend to the whole of our personality. This necessarily involves surrendering our whole lives to Jesus Christ by accepting him as our Lord and

Savior. In this act of surrender and commitment, we receive a deeper faith conviction and knowledge concerning the reality and majesty of Jesus Christ, the Lord, the Son of God.

Then because we have accepted within our lives that full work of Christ, "The sacrament of faith" (baptism) can begin to produce fruit in a life of holiness worthy of God. That is why Paul said, "Knowing this: our old man was co-crucified so that the body of sin might be rendered impotent in order that we no longer be slaves to sin" (Rom 6:6). It is impossible to describe with mere words what good news this really is.

A young woman in one of my theology classes heard me teach on this Scripture passage about the old man being crucified and came up after class. She asked: "Do you really mean that I can be free of sin that besets me?" When I answered "Yes," the woman explained that since she had been a little child, she had seen great cruelty in her home. Her father was an alcoholic and had treated her mother very badly. Because of this, she had such resentment in her heart toward her father that she did not feel free to approach Holy Communion. She saw no way that she could ever be free of these feelings of bitterness, anger, and resentment.

I urged her to turn her life over to Jesus Christ and to claim the saving power of his cross. It was power which her faith, a work of God within her, and her baptism, equally a work of God in her, had mediated to her. The young woman began every day to pray very peacefully and quietly, and to turn this area of her life over to Jesus Christ.

Within a few months, she saw the truth. She saw that in her as well, "The body of sin had been rendered impotent." She was free of this negative and death-dealing attitude. She was able to forgive her father and to receive the Eucharist in deep peace and tranquility of heart.

This is good news for all of us. The cross renders the old man powerless (Rom 6:6). Through the death of Jesus, God condemned sin in the flesh. He rendered it powerless because Jesus died and was freed of all the forces of evil. The same reality occurs in our lives when we are united with Jesus in his death. When we allow the Holy Spirit to apply the power of the cross to our lives, we experience the true powerlessness of sin.

The cross is total submission. Jesus gave himself over to the

Father in the desire to set us free. Submission of our wills to the will of God is the only way we too are able to crucify the flesh.

The cross is a completely selfless act—the only such act in human history. "For our sake he made him sin who knew no sin, so that in him we might become the righteousness of God" (2 Cor 5:21 RSV). Jesus was subject to the sin which so entangles all of us, and yet he lived a life free from any personal sin.

On the cross, Jesus took upon himself all the sins of humanity. Then he turned his back on it. He totally gave himself over to the Father, and in so doing stripped the world's principalities of their power. Under Satan, the whole drive of the human race had been totally self-centered. Jesus reversed that. Through him, through the power of the cross, men and women can be completely given over to God.

We have a divine person within us—a divine person working out death to sin and life to God. Do you experience this marvelous reality? This is the heart of our salvation. Believe it.

WINNING THE VICTORY

Do you ever feel like your life is a record, playing the same old songs over and over again? Sin has cut its own grooves in every one of us. We all have these patterns or structures of sin in our lives. They enslave us and those around us because, as we have seen, structures of sin involve our relationships with others.

The plain fact is, however, that the Lord *does* want to change our lives and the lives of those with whom we live and have to do. Our acknowledgment and confession of sin need not be an embarrassing repetition in which we acknowledge, over and over, the same disordered habits and tendencies. No, the power of the cross of Jesus Christ, uniting us with his body through baptism, by a faith enlivened in the Holy Spirit, can actually change our lives. The power of the cross can give us an inner, living experience of the presence and power of Christ within us. This becomes the source of our confidence, joy, freedom, and assurance in the Holy Spirit. Having that precious pledge of eternal salvation, we can know already in this life what it means to be free from those things which hold us in bondage.

The Holy Spirit will show us the ways in which we habitually fall short of his glory. God is able to use the small and ordinary events in our daily lives to show us our sin, our lack of love, our tendency to protect ourselves. When we express our impatience by yelling at our son who just spilled his milk, we can see our sin. When we selfishly refuse to lend our lawnmower to a neighbor in need, we can see our lack of love. When we put on a false mask and hide our weaknesses, we can see our self-protection.

The good news is not that we have to keep struggling, but that we can surrender ourselves to the cross and have those patterns or structures of sin put to death. So many times, a person is told "Just keep trying. Hope for the best." Do we believe that the Son of God died just so we could muddle through? Jesus can set us free by the power of the cross.

The first step toward appropriating the power of the cross is to accept the fact that we are sinners. We are called to a life of daily repentance: confessing our sins to the Lord and turning away from sin. Repentance is acceptance of the simple truth that we have fallen short of God's glory. We don't have to evaluate the exact degree of blame every time we see an area of sin. Just repent! Take it to the cross and be done with it, especially with a pattern of sin in your life.

The next step is the most important. We need to make a decision: an inward determination to turn an area of sin over to the power of the cross. How much easier it seems to heroically battle sin ourselves and suffer a defeat every now and again! How many of us overindulge at the table, and then diet to lose the same twenty pounds over and over again? We seem to think that if we can avoid completely surrendering ourselves to God, at least our sin will still be around if we ever want it again! If we give in to the cross, our sin is dead, it's finished. Then God can begin to build healthy structures of grace into our lives.

Jesus sent the Holy Spirit to set us free from sin, to take authority over our lives and put sin to death in us. But often we refuse to yield to him and want to fight sin on our own. When we try to overcome sin in our own strength, we grieve the Holy Spirit.

Or even worse, we want to keep our sins and not give them up at all. They can become like old friends after a while, at least comfortable if not always pleasant. These responses grieve the Holy Spirit because he loves us so much. The greatest counselor in the world wants to do so much for us if we will only let him.

The Lord will probably ask you to do some hard things to put to death patterns of sin in your life. He may ask you to find someone whom you can talk to honestly about these matters. You can tell this person frankly, "I'm addicted to this. I'm afraid of that."

The Lord may ask you to probe these sin patterns. "What are the ways that my patterns of thinking lead to sin? What is lurking in my memory to give me a hard time when I least expect it? What are the *occasions and the people* (structures of sin) that call forth the anger, the self-pity, the addiction, the pride that is such a part of me?"

As the Lord speaks to you about these areas of sin, you will need to distinguish the voice of the Spirit from the voice of Satan. It can be difficult to tell the difference, but not impossible. When God speaks about sin, he does it in a way that leads to repentance. He gives us a clear conviction of sin and leads us to purity of heart and inner peace.

When our conscience is being troubled by Satan, he tells us that we are terrible. "You can't change, you might as well give up. You're a failure. There's no good in you," Satan whispers. When thoughts like these trouble you, ask yourself one question: would Jesus Christ ever say that to me? Of course not. Thus you know that the source of these thoughts is the accuser of the brethren.

Rebuke him. Stand on the truth: cleansed by the blood of Christ, you have a perfect right to come before God and praise him. Once you have repented of your sin, learn to spot the lies that drag you down—the temptations to bad self-image, the accusations, the discouragement. We have the right to repent 20,000 times a day and yet still stand confidently in the presence of God.

We don't have to compromise or muddle through life. We can be as free of sin as we want to be. Many psychological problems, as well as oppression, fear, and discouragement reign in our midst because we have not firmly embraced the power of the cross. The power of the cross of Jesus is not just another good idea. It is new life to be lived now by faith in Jesus Christ. It is claiming our spiritual heritage as sons and daughters of God. Pray and beg the Lord to put his cross between you and your sinful flesh. He will do it.

Stand on the cross when the temptation to sin returns. Say, "Look, take it up with the Holy Spirit. He lives in me. Don't bother me with that. I've died to it." If you don't start to fool with the sin again, you will see exactly what Paul means when he says, "Knowing this: our old man was co-crucified so that the body of sin might be rendered impotent, in order that we would no longer be slaves to Sin. For he who has died has been justified in regard to Sin" (Rom 6:6-7).

As we experience greater freedom from the bondage of sin in our lives, will our thinking automatically change? As we learn to control the desires of our flesh, what if our mind continues in rebellion? Deceptive and deceived thinking can sure stir up a lot of trouble. Like the Pharisees, isn't it possible to maintain the appearance of righteousness, and yet be far from the Lord in our minds?

FIVE

Changing Your Mind

D ELVING INTO THE MIND IS LIKE diving into the deepest ocean. We could never discover all of its treasures. Yet those riches are available to us every day. To help us explore the depths of the mind, let me ask you a riddle:

In marbled walls as white as milk,
Lined with a coat as soft as silk,
Within a fountain crystal clear,
A golden apple doth appear.
No doors there are to this stronghold,
Yet thieves break in and steal the gold.

Can you guess the answer? How do we go about solving such a riddle? We use our minds. We employ logic and reason ... and if all else fails, we hope for a flash of intuition. What object does the riddle describe? The egg.

The brain could almost fit this description as well. The marbled walls of a skull are lined with soft but strong membranes. Carefully cradled in cerebral fluid lies a gnarled clump of grayish matter. Though not golden or pretty, it is certainly more precious than gold.

Despite its humble appearance, the brain stores a vast amount of information. Like the conductor of a musical symphony, this internal circuit box governs our most complex movements. Even those simple tasks we take for granted like walking and breathing would be impossible without the proper functioning of the brain.

The *mind* is even more encompassing than the brain. We are created in the image of God. Through the precious gifts of the mind and the spirit, we are able to comprehend the complexities of the universe. God has equipped us with a marvelous capacity to perceive reality, to learn about natural laws, to communicate with him and with others.

Yet thieves break in and steal the gold! Who is the thief? Satan. He has found a hidden doorway *through the flesh* to plunder our minds: "the lust of the flesh, the lust of the eyes, and the pride of life" (1 Jn 2:16 RSV). By undermining our willingness to obey God, he has robbed us of an obedient spirit.

Besides the intellect, men and women possess a free will. In the garden of Eden, Satan planted seeds of doubt and confusion in the mind of Eve concerning the forbidden fruit. Adam and Eve were tempted to find an independent source of wisdom, they sought to know good and evil. But they got more than they bargained for. The biblical meaning of such knowledge, as I mentioned before, is that you can do what you want and that *you* can declare whether it is good or evil. With the knowledge of good and evil came death—alienation from God.

Jesus said that the first commandment is this: "You shall love the Lord your God with all your heart, and with all your soul, and with all your mind, and with all your strength" (Mk 12:30 RSV). But our minds and our hearts are often filled with thoughts and emotions that are not in line with God's truth and love. One of the most important ways we put to death the stubborn flesh in our lives is by winning the battle for our minds.

The Holy Spirit wants to renew our minds so that we are able to be more deeply united with God. Our minds are like a flower garden overgrown with weeds and infested with insects. The master gardener intends to pull the weeds, kill the insects, and prune the plants so they will produce beautiful blossoms.

Or consider another image. Our minds are like a rambunctious Great Dane puppy. Even on a leash, this playful pup is strong enough to pull his master along wherever he wants to go. Pretty soon, the dog has crashed through flower beds, chased frightened poodles, and escaped down the street. Obedience training is necessary to teach this Great Dane some basic commands like "heel," "sit," and "stay." So it is with our minds. God sends the Holy Spirit to help us first to hear his voice and then to obey.

Even though we believe in spiritual realities, how many of us live our lives mostly on a material level? We know we have a master—and in fact we wish to please him—yet the call of the world lures our flesh into dangerous territory. We desire to live one way and end up living another way.

Take a computer analyst who works hard every day and loves his family. He goes to church on Sunday and happily puts a substantial amount into the collection basket. But when Monday dawns, he thinks mostly about how to succeed in the real world—of computers. Everything else takes second place in his life.

The boss asks him to work overtime on a special project. The computer analyst knows that doing so would be wrong in light of his family responsibilities. His teenage son is going through some difficult growing pains and could really benefit from his father's presence at home during the evenings. His wife, stretched to the limit by their son's rebellious attitude, needs extra support as well. But it's difficult to resist the promise of a fat bonus and possible promotion. And, of course, he wants to please his employer. He tells his boss he'll do his best to fit in the extra work, even if it means substantial overtime.

God wants us to choose freely to obey him out of love. When our minds and wills are submitted to God, we are united to God in spirit. By conforming our hearts and wills to the commands of God, we can come to understand him with our minds. Then we can instruct and train our fleshly desires.

The New Testament describes this transformation as *renewal of our minds*: "Put off your former way of life, the old man which is deteriorating through illusory and deceitful desires; to be renewed, rather, in the spirit of your mind" (Eph 4:22-23). Though there is some scholarly dispute over the type of authorship Paul exercised in writing to the Ephesians, for our purposes here it will suffice to abide by the traditional usage. Paul, in writing what he does, is saying that we will not experience the fullness of salvation until our darkened minds are transformed and renewed by the light of the Holy Spirit shining in our spirit.

SPIRIT AND MIND

It is significant that in the passage from the letter to the Ephesians just quoted, the text speaks of the "spirit of your minds." In expressing himself this way, Paul is referring to an aspect of New Testament teaching to which we should pay close attention: the relationship between our spirit and our mind. Understanding that relationship can help us grasp the work of the Holy Spirit in renewing our minds.

First, what do we mean by the mind? That part of the human person which we describe today as "the mind" corresponds more closely to what biblical tradition would call "the heart." This is the place within us where we store memories and ideas and where we make plans and decisions. This is not far from what the first audience of the letter to the Ephesians would have thought as well when they heard the term "mind."

In using the phrase "the spirit of your mind," Paul is expanding that description to include the notion of "spirit" as well as mind. This way of speaking refers to another aspect of New Testament teaching about the work of redemption which, while difficult to understand, is important if we are to grasp what is meant by the renewal and transformation of the mind.

In the deepest part of our being, there is a capacity to be enlivened by God. Very often in his letters, Paul calls this dimension of ourselves our "spirit." The word is very suitable since it reminds us that our spirit is destined to be indwelt by the Holy Spirit. In fact, the new life won for us by the cross of Christ resides fundamentally in our spirit. New Greek-speaking converts to Christianity would recognize the word "spirit" as one used by their philosophers to designate that aspect of a human being that is beyond or deeper than our usual way of imagining and thinking.

When Paul uses the word "spirit," he is acknowledging that there is some truth to this insight of the philosophers. Yet he knows in the light of Christ through his own experience that only through the gift of the Holy Spirit can we be enlivened in our spirit. We have a capacity for God, but no means of fulfilling it. We have no resources to become truly spiritual in the New Testament sense of the term. In fact, when Paul and the rest of the writers in the New Testament use this word, they are not so much teaching us about the structure of the human person as much as they are insisting that there is no new life, no rebirth, no seed of eternal life within us except through the transforming grace of the Holy Spirit giving life to our spirit.

This teaching is repeated again and again in early Christian tradition. Very often, the ancient theologians used the same New Testament term "spirit" to speak of the inner and higher dimension of our existence. They insisted that, at this level, there must be an enlivening action of the Holy Spirit which presides over and is the activating factor within us when we consciously think, will, and act.

Sometimes these early Christian thinkers spoke of this aspect of our being as the "ground" or "high point" of the soul. Or else they spoke of the "higher mind" as opposed to that "lower" functioning of our minds of which we are so conscious in our ordinary life. By this latter they meant that part of the mind which is so disordered by the drives of our emotions and imagination. In any event, the constant witness of early Christian tradition is that something dormant or inactive deep within us must be brought to life by the action of the Holy Spirit. No amount of human energy can accomplish this rebirth. Through this action, we are enabled to become aware of Jesus Christ in a new way and to know God personally as Father, Son, and Holy Spirit.

When we speak, then, of the transformation of the mind, we are talking about that action of the Holy Spirit by which God brings our minds under the power and authority of this new life possessed in the very depth of our personality. The saints have always taught that true Christian prayer and genuine Christian acts are only possible when they flow from a mind and will submitted to this action of the Holy Spirit who dwells within us.

Failure to understand what is meant by a mind submitted to the Holy Spirit leads to much well-intentioned activity that is unable to produce full fruit. For this reason, it is of the utmost importance that we Christians today recover a living and practical knowledge of the working of the Holy Spirit. Then we can discern the source of his movements within us and learn to have our lives submitted to the witness that the Holy Spirit is making to our spirit (see Romans 8:16).

And what does this action of the Holy Spirit accomplish in us?

The first work of the Spirit is to free us from a captive and pagan mindset and bring our minds more fully under the influence of the new life he has given to us in our spirit.

A FANTASY WORLD OF ILLUSION

"This, then, I declare and solemnly attest in the Lord: you must no longer walk as the pagans walk; in the empty futility of their minds, being darkened in their understanding" (Eph 4:17-18). Paul is exhorting the Ephesians in this passage. We can be redeemed—and yet still think as unbelievers do, he warns them.

Most of us can testify to the truth of this from our own personal experience. One minute we can be so touched by the love of God that we know him as our Father. Yet five minutes later, that same mind can be filled with jealousy, anger, stupidity, and distraction. We must take Paul's warning seriously. What, then, are the characteristics of the darkened mind? Let us look in some detail at the passage in Ephesians, chapter four.

> This, then, I declare and solemnly attest in the Lord: you must no longer walk as the pagans walk; in the empty futility of their minds, being darkened in their understanding, alienated from the life of God because of the ignorance that is in them caused by the hardness of their heart. Such people, devoid of any moral sensitivity, have given themselves over to unrestrained self-indulgence, carrying out every sort of impurity with a lust for more. But as for you, it is not thus that you learned Christ,—if you really heard him and were taught in him—as the truth is in Jesus: [that is] to put off your former way of life, the old man which is deteriorating through illusory and deceitful desires; to be renewed, rather, in the spirit of your mind, and put on the New Man, who is according to God, created in the righteousness and holiness of the truth. (Eph 4:17-24)

Paul says that "the pagans live in the empty futility of their minds." "Empty futility" basically means that we don't know why we're alive. We don't know what we're doing. We really don't have any reason to live except that we don't want to die, since "the whole world is held in slavery by Satan because of the fear of death" (Heb 2:15). Futility is the experience of anyone who lives without direction, without purpose, without meaning, without hope. Life may be terrible, but death is worse.

A mind in this condition, Paul says, is "darkened," without any real perception of God. The pagan mind lives in a fantasy world of illusion and deception. Life goes on in an endless turmoil of emotions—fear, anger, vengeance, desire, and lust. There is no God to turn to, no release, no meaning.

People live this way because of "their hardness of heart." They see the truth, but they're too weak or lazy to grasp it. The heart is *hard*, unaffected by the truth. The opposite of a hard heart is one that seeks the truth, that is open to the movement of the Holy Spirit and allows itself to be shaped by the hand of God.

The Book of Exodus gives us the example of Rameses II, who ruled Egypt at the time. Even when confronted by the awesome power of God, Pharaoh's heart was hardened. He refused to listen to Moses or let the people of Israel go.

In the time of Jesus, most of the Pharisees and the Sadducees rejected him as the Messiah because of their hardheartedness. They sensed a threat to their power and traditions, which were of greater concern to them than their relationship with God. Human pride is at work here—a refusal to acknowledge someone greater than one's self. Pilate asked Jesus, "What is truth?" But his question was merely rhetorical. In the face of the embodiment of truth, Pilate pridefully asserted his right to his own opinion.

A hard heart is devoid of any moral sensitivity. In Ephesians, Paul calls this trait "callousness" or "resistance." Pagans have no sensitivity, no judgment, no real grasp of the moral issues. They are busy perpetrating evil against one another and against themselves, and suffering the consequences.

Those who participate in the abortion business provide a good example. The doctors who own and operate abortion clinics have sworn the Hippocratic oath to protect life—yet a lot of money can be made serving women who wish to "terminate a pregnancy." These doctors might rationalize, "Someone will abort these fetuses. Why shouldn't we be the ones to make a good living doing such a simple medical procedure?" People who advocate "freedom of choice" have no real understanding of God's sovereignty and the sanctity of unborn life.

The consequences are enormous. Millions of babies are murdered. Countless women are tormented by guilt and sorrow for years—if not for a lifetime. Sexual irresponsibility is encouraged and "unwanted pregnancies" continue unabated.

Indeed, sexual irresponsibility is one of the surest symptoms of a captive and darkened mind. Paul says:

> Because, knowing God, they did not glorify him as God or give thanks, rather they became devoid of sense in their reasonings and their uncomprehending heart was darkened. Claiming to be wise, they became foolish; and they exchanged the glory of the incorruptible God for the likeness of the image of corruptible man, and of birds and four footed animals and reptiles. Therefore God gave them over, in the desires of their hearts, to uncleanness, for the dishonoring of their bodies among themselves. (Rom 1:21-24)

We see this moral callousness wreaking havoc on the world today, particularly in areas of sexual sin. The current AIDS crisis is largely the result of sexual immorality. In most cases, AIDS leads to death at an early age. An epidemic is predicted for the decade ahead, with no known cure at present.

Unrestrained self-indulgence is an attempt to give meaning to a life without God. We see this prominently displayed in the typical American "Yuppie" lifestyle: make as much money as possible; accumulate possessions to support a life of comfort and leisure; pursue relationships and activities that satisfy physical appetites. But an endless round of experiences and indulgence of desires fails to fill the large void in the human spirit made for God. If left unchecked, this kind of pursuit leads to spiritual death.

This miserable condition of the darkened mind stands in stark contrast to the wisdom possessed by the Christian with a transformed mind. "That is not how you learned Christ," Paul says. That's a marvelous phrase: *learn Christ.* The object of our learning is the man Jesus Christ. Pagans learn darkness and futility. We learn something else—a man like us in all ways but sin.

As we learn Christ, he will transform our minds through the power of his cross and the action of the Holy Spirit.

WE LEARN CHRIST

"But you are a chosen race, a royal priesthood, a holy nation, God's own people, that you may declare the wonderful deeds of him who called you out of darkness into his marvelous light" (1 Pt 2:9 RSV). God floods our beings with his light and clarity. When our minds are transformed, he brings peace, order, and wisdom into our daily lives.

An *enlightened* mind knows important truths about God. It thinks correct thoughts and displays an abundance of spiritual knowledge. In contrast, a *transformed* mind is in touch with Jesus Christ directly by way of a personal relationship.

Learning Christ and putting on the new man is a very down-to-earth, concrete experience. I want to discuss some practical ways in which this transformation occurs:

1. Ponder the Scriptures. Our minds are like sponges. They soak up everything that comes into them. In the course of our normal lives, they become full of illusions, lies, dreams, obsessions, disordered desires, and disconnected fantasies. We must wring out this dirty sponge and wash it clean in the pure water of God's holy Word.

I suggest that you deliberately immerse yourself in the Scriptures. Set aside some time every day solely for reading and studying the Bible. Seek the Scriptures for God's perspective on your condition and his plan for your life. Consider meditating on a verse of Scripture throughout each day. The Word of God has power. Use it. I strongly recommend the periodical, *The Word Among Us*, as a means of meditating on Scripture every day. This periodical is published each month and gives daily meditations on the readings at Mass. To obtain a copy or to subscribe, write *The Word Among Us*, Box 6003, Gaithersburg, MD 20884-9924.

2. Daily Prayer. If we do not pray every day, we are not in touch with God. Prayer is a duty in the same sense that breathing is a duty. If we stop breathing, we will die. If we stop praying, we will shrivel up spiritually and become captive to a darkened mind.

Many good Christians try hard to be nice, but they become very confused because they do not pray. It is easy to go on, day after day, lulled to sleep by the newspaper, the television, and the world around us. Pretty soon, we say, "Maybe these people with all their new ideas are right. After all, even the Scripture scholars don't agree. We'll just wait and see what happens."

To enter into daily prayer, choose a definite time—the best time you have available—and dedicate it solely to prayer. Start out by praying five to ten minutes a day. Commit yourself to it. Choose a place where you are totally free from distractions. Put aside worries and anxieties: don't allow problems to dominate your prayer.

Since many people have difficulty knowing what to do even after they have resolved to pray, let me offer a suggested format for prayer:

a) Enter into the presence of God and repent for your sins. Let the Holy Spirit lead you in a quiet, reflective review of the time since your last prayer. Don't try to go on a "search and destroy" mission. When the Spirit leads you to repent, he will also help you surrender your sin to the power of the cross. It is most important in this context that we learn to repent for the disorder in our minds. There is confusion in our thinking and deceit in our judgments. As we repent for this and beg the Lord to show us how our sinful drives affect the way we think, we will arrive at inner clarity and freedom.

b) Praise and adore the Father, Son, and Holy Spirit for who they are and what they have done for us. It may be helpful to read a psalm of praise out loud or to recite the Creed. Proclaim the glorious truths of your salvation.

c) Listen to God by being attentive to what he wants to say to you. The most effective means of listening to God is prayerfully reading the Scriptures and asking the Lord questions about what you're reading.

d) Finally, intercede for the church, for the spread of the gospel, for heads of government, for the poor and suffering, for your family and friends, for strength for the day and its trials, for protection from evil.

Go before the Lord and beg the Holy Spirit to teach you how to pray. Get on your knees and ask Jesus Christ to guide you. Find a trustworthy priest or a knowledgeable friend in whom you can confide. As you pray, ask the Lord to teach you what it means to die to sin. That is the very essence of what it means to have a transformed mind.

Also, ask God to reveal his love for you. Ask him every day. Tell him that you just don't understand his love, or that you're not able to experience it. Stick with it. There is nothing God wants to reveal to us more than this—that he loves and cherishes us and desires our happiness.

I will make you a promise. As you seek God in daily prayer, your knowledge of how much he loves you will ultimately change your whole personality. In the depth of God's love, we begin to develop a transformed mind. The Lord may have to show you a lot of sin before you can grasp how much he loves you. But once you comprehend his very personal love for you, you will never be the same. That's the incomparable benefit of daily prayer.

3. Be Alert to the Media.   Judge the quality of the information you receive every day. Most Christians are entirely too trusting about television, the secular press, and the media generally. Ask hard and probing questions. What value system is being promoted by this material? Is this movie truly entertaining and refreshing, or is it appealing to an aspect of your personality that is troublesome? Are the books you read contributing to the renewal of your mind, or reinforcing sinful thoughts and desires?

Some people get hooked on television, soap operas, or romantic novels. Are the moral values we see portrayed able to stand in the light of God's truth? How about the quality of the relationships depicted in popular television shows like "L.A. Law" or "Miami Vice"? The accepted norm is to move from one sexual relationship to another, to live together outside of marriage, to place career foremost. Does this reflect committed Christian love?

Use your mind to filter and assess the information that comes into it. Keeping the sponge clean to begin with can be hard work, but easier in the long run. To help in this effort, I would recommend that Christians put a time limit on the amount of media they expose themselves to each week.

4. Gain Authority over Emotions and Desires. The final transformation involves our emotions which govern so much of our behavior. Consider how much our thoughts are pure emotional fantasies. Do you ever find yourself replaying an encounter with someone you are upset with? Let's say a husband comes home from work one day and neglects to ask his wife how her day went. Perhaps he was just distracted by the kids at the dinner table or extremely tired from the day's work.

His wife begins to experience an emotional reaction. As it so happens, she had a very eventful day and was just bursting to tell someone about it. She wonders, doesn't he care? The more she thinks about it, the angrier she feels. If he cares so little, then to heck with it, she decides.

Such pure anger will eat the life out of our hearts like acid. Get rid of thoughts like these, for your own good and for the sake of your relationships. Give the person the benefit of the doubt. Learn to share honestly and not out of a desire for "revenge." Don't call someone's love and concern into question over something so trivial.

Get rid of lustful thoughts, depressed thoughts, fearful thoughts. Extinguish the ego trips and fantasizing that consume your thought lives. Be vigilant about what you allow your mind to dwell upon. Look at the thoughts you have during the day and determine where they come from: the Holy Spirit? the flesh? Satan?

Look at your desires. The surest test of a transformed mind is to examine the sources of our basic desires of joy, grief, hope, and fear. Do you find your joy in your own accomplishments or in the salvation won for you by Christ? Do you grieve over insults or over your own personal sin and that of the world? Do you hope in your success, health, or intelligence—or do you hope in Jesus Christ? Do you fear loss of money or esteem, or do you fear losing your relationship with God?

If your joy, grief, fear, and hope come from yourself, then your desires are based on illusions and fantasies, not on Jesus Christ who is the truth. Be honest. If you see failure or weakness, call it by its right name. Don't be afraid of the truth—seek it and act upon it.

God is there to give you all the grace you need to repent and change.

ALIVE TO GOD

A transformed mind shows itself as an active, disciplined mind. What exactly is an active mind? How does it operate? Let's flesh out our understanding of this important reality by considering the example of John Paul II. Even as a boy, he approached life with a zeal that amazed his family and friends. In school, Karol Wojtyla learned with a passion that continued throughout his life. His enthusiasm for the theater reflected his desire to touch the hearts of people with truth.

After Poland was torn apart by war, Wojtyla's trust in God only strengthened. He developed a deep devotion to prayer, particularly the Rosary, through involvement in the Living Rosary movement and reading St. John of the Cross. This dedication to prayer continued in his struggle against Communism.

As Cardinal of Krakow, Karol Wojtyla repeatedly fought for the freedom of the church under tyranny. One of his priorities was to pester the authorities for permission to build a church in Nowa Huta, a model city designed to be totally atheistic. One morning in 1967, the new cardinal took up a pick axe and started breaking ground himself for the foundation. The new church was dedicated ten years later, in spite of continued government opposition.

When his personal courage and holiness were put to the test by an assassin's bullet, Pope John Paul II visited the cell of the man who had tried to kill him. Embracing and publicly forgiving this man taught the world more than words ever could about the radical power of Christian love and forgiveness.

The first quality of new life in Jesus is just such an active mind—a strong mind that has been touched by revelation so that it is able to understand God's plan of salvation. An active mind is clear, washed in the blood of Jesus Christ, and able to abide confidently in his grace.

However, there is a price to pay. We have given our minds over to many things besides the eternal truths of God. The price we pay is dying to our flesh, dying to our sin, and living to God. The secret to a strong mind is keeping ourselves submitted to the truth: the revelation of God through the cross of Christ. "Therefore gird up your minds, be sober, set your hope fully upon the grace that is coming to you at the revelation of Jesus Christ" (1 Pt 1:13 RSV).

What does that mean, to "gird up your mind"? Or, it could be more precisely rendered, "Gird up the loins of your mind." The image of long, flowing robes is common in many cultures in the Near East, like that of the ancient Jews or traditional Bedouin tribesmen of today. Long robes are an encumbrance when people have to get ready for action. They must hoist up their robes and tuck them under their belts to be ready to work and move.

Jesus spoke of this need for preparation to his disciples: "Let your loins be girded and your lamps burning, and be like men who are waiting for their master to come home from the marriage feast, so that they may open to him at once when he comes and knocks" (Lk 12:35-36 RSV). Be alert; be awake; be ready for action.

The cause for much of our lack of readiness can be found in our minds. What is going to stop the encumbrances, the distractions, the thoughts that can make us stumble and slow us down? The truth. Who is the bearer of this good news to us? The Holy Spirit. He is our counselor day after day. As we accept the witness of the Holy Spirit within us, as we surrender and obey him, our minds are purified by the truth.

An active mind is one that is motivated by the Holy Spirit to know Jesus Christ and his will. St. Thérèse of Lisieux provides a wonderful example of what it means to be alive to God in this way. In her short life, she concentrated so much on learning the ways of God that many notable theologians have studied her teachings.

St. Thérèse was not professionally educated and never studied theology. She died at age 24 as a Carmelite nun, having entered the order at age 15 in spite of rigorous protests from superiors. Where did she learn about God? The Holy Spirit instructed her because she had an active mind, alert to the truths of God.

St. Thérèse's deep hunger for God is reflected in a statement she once made: "If I had been a priest, I should have made a thorough study of Hebrew and Greek so as to understand the thought of

God as he has deigned to express it in our human language." That hunger reflects an active, aggressive mind. Do we have the same expectancy that God will reveal himself to us?

When his knee was crippled by a cannonball, Ignatius of Loyola had time to think. After reading a number of romantic novels, he thought it would be great to be a war hero and have all the girls running after him. But when he read the lives of the saints, he felt another kind of attraction. As he lay in bed, he was able to say something like, "Do you see how stupid I was? Those romantic novels turned me on, but then afterwards I had a bad taste in my mouth. But the lives of the saints got me excited. After I finished reading those stories, I was peaceful and stayed excited." St. Ignatius learned to believe God and to obey him.

Paul says in Romans:

I appeal to you therefore, brethren, by the mercies of God, to present your bodies as a living sacrifice, holy and acceptable to God, which is your spiritual worship. *Do not be conformed to this world but be transformed by the renewal of your mind, that you may prove what is the will of God, what is good and acceptable and perfect.*
(Rom 12:1-2 RSV)

If our minds are still captive to the drives of the flesh, it is impossible for us to be holy and acceptable to God. The work of the Holy Spirit in our minds brings clarity and light. We know what we're thinking, and we know how to think. If our minds are clear, we're able to know God's will and are truly alive. To know the will of God is a priceless gift. To do the will of God is even better.

CAUGHT IN A STORMY CONFLICT

Because the mind is most often the battleground where we win or lose in the Christian life, the heart of our salvation lies precisely in having a transformed mind. Most Christians fight a pitched battle in their thoughts all the time, and try to scrape through on willpower. But we're often confused about the real issues, manipulated by Satan, and victimized by the stormy conflict with temptations. In the end, we might pull off a victory and win the game in overtime with a score of 106 to 105. But we do so at a terrible price, and we completely miss the fullness of God's plan for us.

A wife who has to juggle housework and career outside the home is tempted to feel sorry for herself. She works hard at the office all day, and then rushes home to prepare a delicious dinner. Her children and her husband don't seem to appreciate her.

The woman who lives across the street resists getting a job so that she can make homemaking a bigger priority. But her husband and children seldom comment on how clean and inviting the house is. Meanwhile, the magazines she reads trumpet how a woman can't be fulfilled unless she has a career outside the home.

Her husband, the sole breadwinner, is tempted to feel sorry for himself. He has to get up very early and drive an hour to work every morning, only to face a nagging boss who gives him unrealistic deadlines. It seems he can never catch up. His wife and his children rarely thank him for bringing home a paycheck every week. He sees his neighbors and friends having an easier time and thinks, "There must be an easier way to make a living. Life should be more fun."

A college student has given her life to the Lord, but is confused by what she hears in class. Her philosophy professor sounds so convincing when he talks about our inability to know God, moral relativism, and the superiority of logic. How does all of this fit in with her Christian beliefs? Her boyfriend tells her she's being old-fashioned about refusing to have sex. He says everyone's doing it, and they're not being struck down by a bolt of lightning. Whom should she believe?

This kind of battle can go on in our minds all day. We can all be involved in some very difficult or even dangerous situations, but the real spiritual fight is waged within and over our minds. Do we notice what we do with our minds? Would a mother and father stand watching calmly as their two-year-old daughter runs out into a city street bustling with traffic? No! They would keep a firm hold of her hand and take care to protect her from danger.

We need *vigilance.* The New Testament repeatedly uses the Greek word *gregorein* to describe the attitude of being alert and watching, like a shepherd. Jesus used graphic illustrations like that of a man of position and wealth going away and then coming back unexpectedly to find out how well his servants have managed his household.

Another parable speaks of the thief who breaks in to steal our most valued possessions. If we knew when the thief was coming, we would wait up for him. We would be alert. We would not let him come in and rob us.

The most remarkable text that discusses vigilance is the account of the agony in the garden. In Mark 14:34, Jesus says to Peter, James, and John, "My soul is very sorrowful, even to death; remain here, and watch." Luke tells us that the suffering of Jesus in the garden of Gethsemane was so intense that his sweat became like great drops of blood (Lk 22:44). He prays that this cup would pass from him, "yet not my will, but your will be done."

Jesus was vigilant during this intense conflict in the garden. That is, his mind was set upon the purposes of God; he focused on identifying his will with that of his Father and fully cooperating with the Father's plan for his life—in spite of the physical suffering that lay before him.

Once this basic decision of his will had been resolved, Christ went to his death with great dignity. The physical suffering he endured was unimaginable: the cruel whipping, being crowned with thorns, carrying his cross through the streets of Jerusalem, having nails driven through his hands and feet, hanging upon the cross. Yet Jesus had already endured the most intense suffering—and won his victory—in the garden. The key to victory was his attitude of heart and mind—his commitment to doing the will of his Father—which was settled in Gethsemane.

On the other hand, the disciples failed their test of vigilance. When Jesus returns to find his waiting disciples asleep, he says, "Simon, are you sleeping? Could you not be on the watch one hour? All of you, be on the watch and pray that you do not come into temptation. The spirit is eager, but the flesh is weak" (Mk 14:37-38). Jesus is faced with his ultimate spiritual battle—one of the mind and will. He is asking for the prayer support of his most intimate circle of friends, but they fail to recognize the significance of his request.

Jesus is calling *us* to be on guard and stay awake.   A battle is raging around us. We need to pray that we will not be put to the test. If we do not let our spirit be subject to the Holy Spirit, we are going to fall asleep. For Mark, *sleep* is a very powerful word. It means to succumb to the power of Satan, to be in a stupor, not to know what is going on.

We can pretend that the battle in our minds isn't really going on—or even if it is, that it isn't all that serious. Or we can look at our consciences and obtain godly self-knowledge. We can spot sinful or disordered thoughts as soon as they arrive and put them to death through the power of the cross. We can see where Satan is at work and rebuke him in the name of Jesus Christ.

Examination of Conscience.   A powerful aid in maintaining what First Peter calls a "sober mind" can be found in the Catholic tradition of examination of conscience. By this I do not mean introspection—that struggle of the flesh to find out what is wrong. Introspection can be very discouraging. We can hardly ever see what is really wrong, and we certainly can't fix it.

Christian examination of conscience is a work of the Holy Spirit—born of the acknowledgment that our hearts are rebellious, and that by ourselves we can do nothing but sin (see Romans 14:23). We should review our lives in an orderly way to see where we have failed to be obedient to God's commandments. Have we been faithful to the duties of our state in life? Have we kept the commands of the church like weekly attendance of Mass?

Basically, we are looking at our lives with the guidance of the Holy Spirit and asking, "Where have I sinned?" This honest self-appraisal prepares us to turn to the Lord who brings his mercy into our lives. The fruit is *self-knowledge* that comes through revelation. God will show us what is wrong. And he will fix it.

There are only two reasons why we should have a troubled conscience. One is sin. The second is harassment by Satan. If we have sinned—fallen prey to one of the many weaknesses of our flesh—we are troubled because we are guilty. That gnawing sense of guilt comes from the Holy Spirit because of unrepented sin. The solution is to repent and be at peace. The Spirit never points out an area of sin in our lives and leaves us without any sense of how to overcome it.

Satan is the accuser of the brethren. Guilt accompanied by embarrassment or self-hatred is the work of the enemy. If the evil one is manipulating our emotions and harassing us with wicked thoughts, we should rebuke him—and be at peace.

We need to *form* our consciences as well as follow them. We need to know whether we have sinned so that we can repent when we have, and resist the accusations of the evil one when we haven't. Being tolerant of sin in our lives is wrong. A harried mother might think, "I was in a bad mood and yelled at the kids all day, but supper was on the table on time." A man or a woman at the office might think, "I gave in to lustful thoughts today, but I got my report done."

Do you see the deception here? Good works don't balance out sin. Our consciences are clouded, swayed like an unjust judge by all sorts of bribes. However, as the Holy Spirit purifies us, our consciences become like a just judge who can rightly evaluate our thoughts. We bring them to the cross, submit them, and repent when they are evil. We should not live with a troubled conscience.

There is a marvelous passage from Diadochos of Photiki, a bishop of the early church, which likens a purified mind to a tranquil sea (from "On Spiritual Knowledge," by St. Diadochos of Photiki in *The Philokalia* I, compiled by St. Nikodimos of the Holy Mountain and St. Makarios of Corinth, Faber and Faber, Boston, 1986 reprint, pp. 259-60):

Those pursuing the spiritual way must always keep the mind free from agitation in order that the intellect, as it discriminates among the thoughts that pass through the mind, may store in the treasuries of its memory those thoughts which are good and have been sent by God, while casting out those which are evil and come from the devil.

When the sea is calm, fishermen can scan its depths and therefore hardly any creature moving in the water escapes their notice. But when the sea is disturbed by the winds, it hides beneath its turbid and agitated waves what it was happy to reveal when it was smiling and calm; and then the fishermen's skill and cunning prove vain.

Do you see why the world, the flesh, and Satan want to keep us agitated in our minds—running all the time, trying, hoping that good works will satisfy that gnawing sense of isolation and sin? The Lord doesn't want that. We need to stop, face it, and put it to death. Diadochos continues:

> Only the Holy Spirit can purify the intellect, . . . In every way, therefore, and especially through peace of soul, we must make ourselves a dwelling-place for the Holy Spirit. Then we shall have the lamp of spiritual knowledge burning always within us; and when it is shining constantly in the inner shrine of the soul, not only will the intellect perceive all the dark and bitter attacks of the demons, but these attacks will be greatly weakened when exposed for what they are by that glorious and holy light.

Diadochos accurately described the battle in our mind and the choice we have. It is not in our power to decide whether we are to be disturbed by our thoughts. But it is up to us to decide if they are to linger within us, and whether or not they are to stir up our passions.

The Lord surely intends to give us victory in our minds. As our minds become clear and active, how can we learn more about walking under the authority of the Holy Spirit? What can we look for in our lives to see the fruit of submission? It's so easy to be deceived and to think that everything is fine—when in reality, we could be headed for a big fall. What does God really expect of us, mere creatures made of dust and full of weakness?

SIX

Step by Step with the Holy Spirit

A WILDERNESS ENTHUSIAST BAR NONE, suppose you have saved money for years to pursue the ultimate adventure. Suppose you are in the Australian outback roughing it with a friend. Your friend is bitten by a poisonous snake and you are unable to extract all the venom. You quickly size up the gravity of your situation.

You've hiked onto rough terrain by foot and are still a couple of days from your rendezvous with civilization—a sizable town with a hospital.

What can you do to save your friend's life?

Then you remember that you passed a large ranch about six miles back and had noticed horses grazing nearby—but no sign of any cars. The task had seemed impossible only minutes before, but now you have a fighting chance of borrowing one of the rancher's horses and going for help in time to save your friend's life.

You may be thinking, what does this story have to do with following the Holy Spirit step by step?

Well, in some respects, the Holy Spirit is like the rancher's horse which you so desperately need to borrow. Only, in the case of the Holy Spirit, we are talking about an eternal and priceless partnership and not simply a one-time service. Consider, for instance, that the horse will give you the power to reach your destination in time in a life-and-death matter—or so you *hope*. Yet while the horse will carry you there, you must exert some effort as well by riding the horse. In spite of tiredness and soreness, you must *continue* to ride the horse if you are to get medical help in time to save your friend's life. Just so with the Spirit. He provides us with the spiritual power to carry us through our Christian life and on into heaven—the one life-and-death journey that ultimately counts. But we, for our part, must stay tapped into the power and grace the Holy Spirit offers us. Some effort is required by us, but the power comes from God.

Or consider another example—this time from the writings of St. Thomas Aquinas. Suppose you are out in the ocean far from shore in a rowboat. You are rowing to shore when you realize, in despair, that you are never going to make it.

Then suppose the Lord arrives on the scene and rigs up a sail in your rowboat. Now, because you have the sail, the wind can carry you back to shore—something that would have been impossible on your own meager resources. Thus, we see how God must provide us with the resources we simply do not possess if we are to arrive at our goal—without him, we are lost and adrift at sea with no hope of rescue.

Walking in the Holy Spirit is something like riding a horse or sailing a ship. The power comes from outside ourselves, but we must cooperate with it. It is here, however, that our analogy breaks down. While riding a horse or sailing a ship, we remain essentially unchanged. But our journey to heaven in the power of the Holy Spirit necessarily implies a personal transformation.

By the grace of God, this transformation will be accomplished and we will arrive safely at paradise. When we come to Christ, we enter into a life of power and direction. The Spirit is empowering the vessel of our earthly bodies to give us a capacity for holiness far beyond our own resources.

Better yet, the Spirit actually dwells within us to be our counselor and guide. By walking in the Spirit, we are able to live up to the expectations of God our Father. It isn't enough to have an active and renewed mind. We must exercise our mind under the Spirit's authority. Just sitting and thinking correct thoughts is not enough either. We must learn to walk in the Spirit.

WHO'S IN CHARGE?

So who's in charge? The flesh or the Spirit? That is the struggle we face every day, until we reach paradise. God wants to lead and guide us. Otherwise, why bother to listen and discern? If God does not lead us personally, then the best thing to do is just to sit down and figure out what seems best to us, then carry on. But that's not the Christian life.

The basis of our life is a personal relationship with the Lord of the universe, Jesus Christ. Through Jesus, we have access to the captain of the ship. Only God has the navigational skills to keep us on course. Jesus will undertake the direction of our lives if we will learn to be submissive to him.

Submission is a word that immediately makes our flesh rebel! We somehow have this notion that surrender is for cowards. The flesh wants to be in charge, and can usually put up a good argument for doing things its way. We are easily pushed around by our desires. Even when we get what we think we want, the flesh is usually quick to point out why it's not quite enough!

God does not promise to satisfy all of our desires. The point of the Christian life is not to live happily ever after, at least in this imperfect world. Actually, we may face a good amount of suffering in some form or another.

What God does promise is that he will satisfy our deepest longings by our relationship with the Father of life himself. Even so, we won't be completely satisfied until we are able to see God face to face in heaven. Our mind and spirit need to know that only the vision of God is going to make us truly happy and only by possessing the Holy Spirit will we come to know that happiness. To convince our stubborn flesh of that truth is the work of the Holy Spirit.

If we let Jesus establish his lordship over us, then we will know what it means to live under the authority of the Holy Spirit. God says, "Be holy. Belong to me. Put me first. Put me on the throne of your life. Worship and adore me. Obey me. Don't be afraid of other people, but fear me. I have authority. I can't be bought off. It is because of me that you have life. I'm on your side."

Holiness is a high calling. Who can do it? On our own power, we can do nothing but bring about our eternal death. Some folks try to avoid displeasing God, but essentially live their lives in a way that pleases themselves. There is a big difference between that approach, and living a life totally pleasing to God. Really having God's intentions and desires foremost requires a total reorientation of our lives:

> *"Be sober,* set your hope fully upon the grace that is coming to you at the revelation of Jesus Christ. As obedient children, do not be conformed to the passions of your former ignorance, but as he who called you is holy, be holy yourselves in all your conduct." (1 Pt 1:13-15 RSV)

What does it mean to *be sober*? First, it means quite literally to be sober, not addicted to alcohol. Most people would say, "But I'm not an alcoholic." Maybe you're not. But if we experience that kind of distraction and cloudiness of mind on a regular basis, then our lives are to some extent out of order. We are expressing in our own way a desire for confusion. In other words, we are avoiding the purity and clarity of the truth. Let us be sober.

But the word in Greek, as in English, has a much broader meaning. It means to *be under authority.* We must be under the Holy Spirit's authority. If we are not surrendered to God's authority, we will be under the control of something else or someone else. And anything else or anyone else does not want the best for us.

When the flesh is in control, what are some of the impulses that dominate us? Consumption of too much food or alcohol are significant problems for many people. Other people are compulsive shoppers who are easily tempted to buy things they don't need. Every time a catalogue comes into the house, they read it and want a new electronic gadget or a new dress. They can hardly go into a department store without coming out having bought something.

To be "sober" means we do not just react every time something presents itself to us. Left to our own impulses, we are very self-indulgent. In today's world of instant gratification, comfort can become a top priority.

Many of us go through our days in a random, mindless confusion. Instead of resolutely fulfilling our responsibilities, we are pushed around by the opportunities and desires of the moment. We waste too much time with a long chat in the office. We don't pray because it's too tempting to stay in bed an extra half hour.

Perhaps we give in to the desire to be in control or to run around being busy. Sobriety does not mean running around trying to solve every problem we see. Do we set our goals every morning when we pray, or do we live our days simply responding to what comes our way? It is easy to be consumed by the cares of the world—family, friends, work, and daily news brought to us through the media. There are only so many hours in the day, and the demands placed on us invariably require more time than we have.

Did you ever think about why you do what you do each day? At the top of our emotional list are usually the things we like to do, what we are good at, what we get a kick out of, what feeds our egos.

At the bottom of our list are the things we do not like to do, what is hard for us to do—unless we don't have any choice. And then we tend to grumble and complain, and do what has to be done half-heartedly. Many people live that way all week—waiting for the weekend when they can have fun.

Thus, we are not sober. We are dominated by impulse. To be under the authority of the Holy Spirit means to be responsive to a whole new system of values. The First Letter of Peter explains some of these new values:

> The end of all things has come near. Act intelligently and be self-controlled with a view to prayer. Above all, keep your love for one another enthusiastic, for love covers over a multitude of sins. (1 Pt 4:7-8)

God tells us that the end of all things has come near. What does this mean? It sounds like a whole different perspective. Aren't those guys who wear a billboard proclaiming "THE END IS NEAR" a bit crazy?

The *end* in the New Testament means the *final stage* in God's plan of salvation. It is the end of one era and the beginning of another. It is the end of the age of the flesh. Jesus Christ ushered in the reign of the kingdom of God. His death on the cross ended the reign of the flesh.

The confusion is that we still live in the old era, but we live in it as citizens of a whole new way of life. Paul speaks in terms of groaning with longing:

> For we know that all the creation is groaning together and is in travail together up to now. Not only that: we ourselves, having the first fruits of the Spirit, we ourselves are groaning within ourselves, awaiting sonship, the redemption of our bodies.
>
> (Rom 8:22-23)

Paul knew that when Jesus rose from the dead, the last times had obviously begun. He thought Jesus would surely return soon. However, the primary consideration of "the end of the age" is not chronological. It is the form of this world as we know it which is passing away (1 Cor 7:31).

We live in a period full of *hope*—the time between what has been already accomplished and what has not yet been made fully manifest. "But a seen hope is not a hope; who hopes for what he sees? If then, we hope for what we do not see, we are awaiting in steadfast endurance" (Rom 8:24-25).

So, while we wait, we are cautioned to exercise discipline and self-control. But just keeping a tight reign on our flesh and thinking correct thoughts are not enough. We are above all to be governed by love—God's top priority according to this new system of values in the kingdom of heaven.

The Holy Spirit within us enables us really to love God and our neighbor. Most of us find it most difficult to love the people closest to us—family members or roommates or co-workers who significantly affect our daily lives. To be governed by love requires us to put others first.

In a large family, the father may have a long workday. Yet he may need to rise earlier in the morning to take time for prayer, and then spend time with his children at the end of the day, even though he's exhausted.

His wife needs to be sensitive to his need for peace and order in the house, even though she may be just as tired from a long day's work. An expression of love on her part may be making sure the children pick up all their toys before he arrives home.

The expression of love in an office situation may not be so personal, but is nonetheless just as real. If an administrative secretary is passed over for a promotion she feels she deserves, it's easy to be offended. Even if she was treated unfairly, she still needs to be kind and considerate to the person who received the promotion instead. The kind of cutthroat competition seen in the world has no place in this new system of kingdom values.

As citizens of a new kingdom—under the authority of the King of kings—we must not get our values from this passing age. Worldly thinking uses a reference point bounded by the limits of our life on earth. But we are only pilgrims, passing through on our way to paradise. All that we think and do is related to our eternal destiny as children of God, created to glorify God in all things.

This vision of the nearness of the end of the ages gives the proper perspective to this world. We are set free to serve others in a way that is committed, energetic, and clear-sighted. Without such a vision, our efforts run the risk of arising from a desperate fear that things are never going to change anyway.

We won't be able to minister to the needs of others unless we clearly understand how different the kingdom of God is from the kingdom of the world. We won't be able to care for our spouse, our children, our friends unless we have the spiritual sensitivity and wisdom to understand their real needs. Understanding the eternal dignity and destiny of every person allows us to love others truly.

When Paul says that "the time is short," he is right. Time is short for all of us. Not many of us will be alive in fifty years. It is urgent that we learn how to be obedient to God, so that we can be fruitful for him now and live with him forever. The Lord wants to lead us and guide us by the action of the Holy Spirit in our lives.

The lives of the saints are filled with the Lord's communication to them. Sometimes, it's dramatic. Jesus said to St. Francis, "Francis, my church is a wreck, as you can see all around you. Build it up." Francis was so obedient, he gathered rocks and started rebuilding the physical church in which he was praying. Because he obeyed, he received insight into what the Lord really meant when he told him to build up his church throughout the world of his time.

Our obedience to the Lord can often result in personal suffering and hardship. Paul encourages us with the thought that the sufferings we now experience are not worth comparing with the glory to be revealed to the sons of God:

> For we know that if the earthly tent we live in is destroyed, we have a building from God, a house not made with hands, eternal in the heavens. Here indeed we groan, and long to put on our heavenly dwelling. . . . For while we are still in this tent, we sigh with anxiety; not that we would be unclothed, but that we would be further clothed, so that what is mortal may be swallowed up by life. He who has prepared us for this very thing is God, who has given us the Spirit as a guarantee.
>
> (2 Cor 5:1-5 RSV)

The whole work of the Holy Spirit is to bring us into an eternal union with God. If we learn to live under the authority of the Holy Spirit, we will be able to enter into eternity even now.

PURIFIED BY FIRE

We humans are very shortsighted. We sometimes have trouble making plans for the day. With great effort, we try to plan our career and provide for our children's education. Financial planning enables us to look forward to retirement. But when we plan our future, do we remember to take eternal life into account? We know that one day we will die—but it always seems like such a long way off.

It actually makes more sense to start from the eternal end when we think about our plans and dreams for the future. Eternity makes this part of our existence insignificant in comparison. This pilgrimage is over in a few years; life after death goes on forever.

Eternal life is the real basis of our dignity as human beings, created in the image of God. As we prepare ourselves for eternity, our priorities should change. Eternity begins now. We begin to view our lives not in terms of personal comfort and satisfaction, but rather in terms of God's call to love and serve others.

The Holy Spirit opens the door to a whole new dimension of spiritual reality. By the power of the Spirit, we begin to establish order in our daily lives that properly reflects this eternal perspective. The wisdom of God helps us to understand the extent of our spiritual poverty. What is really important and lasting comes more clearly into focus.

Our lives are like a refinery where precious metals such as gold are purified. We see impurities in our lives each day that need burning up. When we are baptized in the Holy Spirit or experience personal spiritual renewal, we begin to be baptized in fire. The fire of the Holy Spirit is applied to the contents of the smelting pot for the purpose of refinement. The impurities are burned up so that the pure gold remains.

God is trying to bring us to spiritual maturity. Hebrews says that the *mature* are "those who have their faculties trained by practice to distinguish good from evil" (Heb 5:14 RSV). Holiness and maturity as sons and daughters of God become attainable goals by the grace of God.

To grow up in the Lord means to be *strengthened in the inner man*. Paul uttered this prayer on behalf of all those who know Christ:

> For this reason I bend my knees to the Father from whom every family, in heaven and on earth, is named that he give to you, in keeping with the riches of his glory, to be strengthened with power through his Spirit unto the inner man; that Christ dwell, through faith, in your hearts, rooted and grounded in love; so that you may be strong enough to comprehend, with all the saints, what [is] the width and length and height and depth; thus to know the love of Christ surpassing knowledge, that you may be filled unto all the fullness of God. (Eph 3:14-19)

The fullness of God is Christ. God's intention for all eternity is that we be filled with Christ. But the only way that can happen is if we are first emptied out. We are like jugs of muddy water which God wants to fill instead with the wine of gladness. The Holy Spirit shows us how to empty the muddy water out of our minds and hearts, and then fills us with the pure wine of the Spirit.

It is important to notice in this passage that *knowledge* is linked with *strength*. Paul prays that "you be strengthened with power through his Spirit unto the inner man ... so that you may be strong enough to comprehend."

In other words, we are too weak in our human condition even to comprehend God's plan of salvation, much less to lay hold of it and claim it for ourselves. If our minds are filled with ideas from the world, it is fruitless to imagine that we are going to grow in the Christian life. When we are born again, we receive new eyes that perceive spiritual realities. We receive the spirit of wisdom by which God reveals himself to us.

What is the *inner man*? The concept occurs two other times in the New Testament: "So we do not lose heart. Though our outer man is wasting away, our *inner man* is being renewed every day" (2 Cor 4:16 RSV). The other passage reads: "For I delight in the law of God, according to the *inner man*; but I see another law in my members warring against the law of my reason and making me captive to the law of Sin which is in my members" (Rom 7:22-23).

Our *inner man* is that part of us which is capable of being enlivened by the Holy Spirit. It is the deepest part of what Paul calls "the mind" in the text in Romans. Elsewhere, Paul speaks of this same reality as "the spirit." Modern psychology has offered valuable insights, but sometimes fails to take into account this inner nature. Until our spirit is awakened, we don't really know all that a human being is supposed to be. Once awakened, our inner mind or our spirit must be strengthened by the work of the Holy Spirit.

As our spirit comes alive, we begin to experience the rest of our personality being put into proper order. That is what it means to be strengthened in the inner man—to have our lives put in order and our minds expanded and invigorated so that we are able to understand the truth.

As we are gradually set free from habit patterns of sin, we grow in this knowledge of the human situation and what God has done about it. There is no genuine spiritual knowledge without the work of the cross freeing us from sin.

Therefore, our own lives are the laboratory where we experiment with the realities of God and come to know them for ourselves. We come to *know* the fall of the human race. We come to *know* the free gift of salvation. We come to *know* what it means to be called from darkness to light, from death to life. We come to *know* what it means that the Spirit strengthens our inner nature.

Walking in the Holy Spirit yields this deep and personal experience of the eternal truths of God.

BEARING FRUIT FOR GOD

Paul uttered this prayer on behalf of all those who seek to follow Christ:

> And so, from the day we heard of it, we have not ceased to pray for you, asking that you may be filled with the knowledge of his will in all spiritual wisdom and understanding, to lead a life worthy of the Lord, fully pleasing to him, bearing fruit in every good work and increasing in the knowledge of God.
>
> May you be strengthened with all power, according to his glorious might, for all endurance and patience with joy, giving thanks to the Father, who has qualified us to share in the inheritance of the saints in light. (Col 1:9-12 RSV)

We need the power of the Holy Spirit to endure hardships with joy. We especially need knowledge and wisdom to know the mind of Christ and to bear fruit for God. It is very easy today to spend billions of dollars to improve the welfare of the poor—with very little result. Yet think of one indomitable, little old lady, Mother Teresa, in India, who has turned the whole world upside down because she listens to God. St. Francis Xavier baptized a million people in his life, but in himself he was a broken, humble man.

It is not that the Lord does not want things to happen. It is rather that our egos get in the way. This is the area where we are not sober. We love to do things or solve problems because it makes us feel good.

Consider the example of a priest who is sent to Borneo as a missionary. God wants to reveal his mercy and love to the people who live there, but the priest has a plan of action already in mind. He establishes a medical clinic, sets up a school for the children, and helps the people improve their agricultural production.

He is proud to have accomplished so many good things and solved some of their basic problems. While these are certainly worthwhile projects, the priest forgets to listen to the Lord about how to win their hearts for Christ. The eternal gain is sacrificed because of preoccupation with social progress.

We need to learn to hear the Lord clearly directing us in how to serve those in physical, emotional, or spiritual need. When a Christian whose mind has been purified by the blood of Christ undertakes such work, the gospel is preached and the face of Christ is shown forth. But when someone does not live under the authority of the Holy Spirit, the result is a confused effort easily frustrated by the forces of the world.

We need to judge the source of an act, not just how well it turns out. Because of our struggle with sin, it often happens that we produce good works out of our own energy. The pure work of the Holy Spirit is not prompting these actions. Much of what we do comes out of a mixture of human emotion, vanity, sin, pride—and it produces human fruit. Such fruit does not last. It has a tendency to rot.

The saints provide examples for us of fruit that lasts. They were totally submissive to the Lord. Their good works were done out of obedience to Christ, not because they were good things to do. Their lives were totally given over to the sanctifying work of the Holy Spirit as their counselor. They knew how to walk in the Spirit.

Peter Claver, a Jesuit missionary to South America, was such a servant. Calling himself "the slave of the Negroes," he dedicated his life to serving the slaves shipped from West Africa to Cartagena, South America's principal slave market in the early 1600s. Despite fierce opposition from local officials, Peter defended, educated, and baptized over three hundred thousand black slaves. In a courageous display of total self-abandonment, he entered a leper colony daily and cleansed the wounds of the worst victims. The lepers themselves cursed him, but Peter Claver continued faithfully to show them the love of God. He was declared a saint in 1888.

To be sanctified by the Holy Spirit means to be set apart for God. We are freed from sin so that we can become efficient in holiness. "But we have this treasure in earthen vessels, to show that the transcendent power belongs to God and not to us" (2 Cor 4:7 RSV).

By the power of the Holy Spirit, we are delivered "from the dominion of darkness and transferred to the kingdom of his beloved Son, in whom we have redemption, the forgiveness of sins" (Col 1:13-14 RSV). We are delivered from this world in which the principle of existence is death and decay—rotting fruit in other words. What is death? It is disordered energy, energy not brought into proper order by the grace of God.

To be holy is to be free to live a life of ordered energy. God's grace is imparted to us by the Holy Spirit who begins to set our lives in order. We are set apart for God, to be fruitful for him. This happens by obedience. Just as with Mary's "yes" to the angel at the annunciation, the Holy Spirit brings into our very spirit the glorious power and transforming energy of the risen Christ.

God will not give his power to those who are not subject to his authority. A small amount of power might be given, but not serious power to build up the body of Christ. The power to upbuild is also the power to destroy. Unless we are really obedient to God, how could he trust us with his awesome, divine power? It would be like giving an atom bomb to a madman.

We do not have to be perfect—only humble servants of God who desire to be made holy by his Spirit. That is the heart of it. To be fruitful for God means being broken and humble. Jesus provides the clearest example of fruitfulness for God through humble servanthood:

Think like this among yourselves, which is [fitting as it was] in Jesus Christ: who being in the form of God did not consider it a thing to be grasped at, this being equal to God; but he emptied himself taking the form of a slave, become in the likeness of man; and in appearance found as a man, he humbled himself becoming obedient to death, death on a cross. And therefore God raised him on high and gave to him the Name which is above every name; so that at the Name of Jesus every knee should bow of those in heaven, and on earth, and under the earth; and every tongue should confess: Jesus Christ is Lord, to the glory of God the Father. (Phil 2:5-11)

We come to understand the only real source of power when we walk in the Spirit—the power of unselfish love personified by Jesus. If we will only humble ourselves in utter brokenness, God's immeasurable power is able to work wonders through our meager efforts.

The Lord is intent on teaching us to rely on him alone. He knows our weakness. That is why he sends us the Holy Spirit to impart wisdom and power. Listen to this prophetic word which was delivered at the closing session of the North American Congress on the Holy Spirit and World Evangelization in July, 1987:

> The Lord says, "I am the Lord, Jesus Christ. I am the foundation that has been laid, and there is no other. But I warn you because I love you, that you can only build on me, the foundation. But if you do not come and lay down your life before me, if you rely on human resources and human emotions and human power, you will build in straw and hay and wood. Then the fire of judgment will come and destroy your life's work. I tell you this because I love you.
>
> "Your efforts may seem splendorous in the eyes of men, but in my eyes, unless you are submitted to me and my word, they can be hay and straw. You will escape the fire of judgment as a man escaping from a burning building. But your work which seems so great can go up in smoke.
>
> "Come to me. I will teach you, if you will submit your lives to me. If you will abandon your reliance on your own power, if you will turn away from relying on your own egos and your own minds and your own resources, I will place you as a glorious stone in my crown.
>
> "You think that you are wise, that you have insight, that you are clothed with power, but I tell you, you are weak and poor and blind. And I tell you because I love you. Come to me, and I will give you the gold of a precious repentance. And with this gold you can buy from me salve for your eyes and you can see. You can buy from me a white garment and you will be splendid in power. You can buy from me, and I will give you the gold of real wisdom. I promise you this.
>
> "Turn. Stop relying on your own power, stop relying on human power. Rely on me and bear fruit for my kingdom."

The Lord knows that we will experience trials and suffering as we seek to obey him. How does he comfort and strengthen us? Why must we go through hardships? Aren't we promised an abundant life in Christ? Doesn't that mean our lives will be full of blessings?

SEVEN

The Greatest Comforter
in the World

A N OLD BEATLES SONG BEGINS with a desperate plea: "Help! I
need somebody. Help! Not just anybody. Help! You know I
need someone. Help! Won't you please, please help me? Please
help me? Help me! Help me!" The cry is so plaintive that it makes
you want to run and help immediately.

Do you know the feeling? Have you ever been lost in the woods,
all alone? Hopelessness quickly sets in when you have no
resources to find your way out. You've lost your compass. A thick
cloud obscures the sun. All you can do is to cry out as loudly as you
can, "*Help!*" You desperately hope someone is near enough to hear
you, but you fear that you are really all alone.

God has not left us all alone, abandoned and without help. In his
farewell to the disciples at the Last Supper, Jesus reassured them,

> "I will not leave you desolate; I will come to you. Yet a little
> while, and the world will see me no more, but you will see me;
> because I live, you will live also. In that day you will know that I
> am in my Father, and you in me, and I in you." (Jn 14:18-20 RSV)

Jesus knew they were sorrowful and troubled about his
departure. He said many things to them on that occasion to
prepare them for the difficulties that lay ahead. He spoke to them

of love and obedience, the vine and the branches, hatred and persecution to come in the world.

Most of all, he kept reassuring them about the coming of the Holy Spirit:

> "I did not say these things to you from the beginning, because I was with you. But now I am going to him who sent me; yet none of you asks me, 'Where are you going?' But because I have said these things to you, sorrow has filled your hearts. Nevertheless I tell you the truth: it is to your advantage that I go away, for if I do not go away, the *Paraclete* will not come to you; but if I go, I will send him to you." (Jn 16:4-7)

The Greek word *parakletos* is also translated as advocate, protector, helper, comforter. The Holy Spirit will comfort them in their loneliness, provide help in time of need, and protect them with knowledge of the truth.

Jesus knew his disciples faced a hostile world bent on their destruction. Rather than have their faith shaken, the disciples needed to stand firm as witnesses to the truth and power of God. Jesus knew they couldn't do this on their own. They were a sad and fearful group after the crucifixion. Jesus told them to wait for "power from on high" (Lk 24:49). The day of Pentecost left them transformed by the power of the Holy Spirit.

We will face trouble and trials even while obediently walking in the Holy Spirit, but Jesus has given us the greatest comforter and counselor in the world. Since we are often under attack from within and without, God sends the Holy Spirit to strengthen us in our weakness and to comfort us in our afflictions. The Comforter provides the sustaining love and power of the risen Christ which enables his disciples to endure hardship and suffering.

WHY ALL THESE TROUBLES?

Sometimes we feel surrounded by trials and difficulties. People insult us, projects in which we have heavily invested fail, we suffer from sicknesses of all kinds, friends desert us, even family members make fun of us. We may say to ourselves, "I'm going this way and everyone else is going that way. Am I crazy?"

These are trials. And they can be tougher. We could be put in jail, have a large sum of money stolen from us, or be seriously injured in an automobile accident. Such things and worse happen to people every day.

The presence of difficulties and trials in our lives is not accidental or without purpose:

> In this you greatly rejoice though just now, for a little while, you have to suffer the distress of many trials so that the genuine proof of your faith, more precious than perishable gold which is put to the proof by fire, may result in praise, glory, and honor when Jesus Christ is revealed. (1 Pt 1:6-7)

The genuineness of our faith does not mean the quality of our *willpower*, but the quality of the work that God is doing in us. These trials will prove to Christians the absolute authenticity of God's work in them.

As we come to faith in Christ, we can expect trials and conflict to follow. "Beloved, do not be surprised at the fiery ordeal which comes upon you to prove you, as though something strange were happening to you" (1 Pt 4:12 RSV).

Jesus sends the Comforter so that we may endure suffering. The Latin word for "comfort" consists of two words, *com* (intensive) and *fortis* (strong). God gives us strength sufficient to endure any suffering. God doesn't intend that we be *comfortable*, but rather *comforted*.

We are even instructed to rejoice when we encounter difficulties, "knowing that tribulation brings about endurance, endurance something that stands the test, something that stands the test hope, and this hope is not put to shame" (Rom 5:3-4). Faith and hope are strengthened in the midst of suffering.

The First Letter of Peter discusses the role of suffering in the Christian life more clearly than any other New Testament writing. The author pursued this theme so directly because he was writing to people in the Roman provinces in about A.D. 60-70 who were undergoing a great deal of persecution.

The early Christians in Asia Minor were often deprived of status and material possessions. If they were brought to court because someone sued them, they surely lost. Their children could not get good jobs. They were laughed at and excluded. Their former friends would not talk to them. These Christians were moving in one direction, while everyone else was moving in another.

They were suffering precisely because their faith in Jesus Christ set them at odds with the lifestyles of the unbelievers around them. They upset the status quo. The pagans who openly embraced immorality, were angered by a living example of holiness. Their consciences were disturbed, and rightly so.

To encourage these Christians, the author of First Peter first appealed to their minds. He encouraged them to hang on to their living knowledge of what Jesus Christ had done for them, so that they could persevere. Their faith was being tested through fire like gold. Peter promised that with hope, they would be able to remain faithful (1 Pt 1:3-5).

They were also called on to win others to Christ by their words and example. Because of their sufferings, the hope that they expressed would be all the more remarkable. They were encouraged not to fight back or try to get even for the abuse they suffered, but rather to answer those who persecuted them with gentleness and reverence. "For it is better to suffer for doing right, if that should be God's will, than for doing wrong" (1 Pt 3:17 RSV).

The Christians of Peter's time were being challenged by the enemies of the gospel—and by the curious who were looking for something to believe in. So are we. Such onlookers—curious or hostile—call us to account for our hope. The hope that is in us is supposed to be obvious.

Married couples who remain faithful even in the face of serious relationship problems provide an example of this kind of enduring hope. They believe that God has joined them together and will help them to resolve their difficulties over time. The world offers divorce as an easy solution, but ignores the power of God—often mediated through others—to overcome problems that seem impossible to hurdle.

We should demonstrate a concrete hopefulness even in the midst of serious difficulties. We do not live for this world only, but for our inheritance in the world to come. Indeed, we are able to embrace God even more purely when we are not motivated by personal pleasure or gain. Whatever trials God permits in our lives are for our spiritual good. Whenever we suffer for the love of God, we are hammering nails into the self-love and self-will of our flesh. Let us pray with a submissive heart, "May your will be done."

THE PARADOX OF POWER

Do you remember the story of Gideon (Jgs 6:36-7:25)? He laid a fleece of wool before the Lord and asked for a promise from God to deliver Israel by his hand. God confirmed his intention by covering the fleece with enough dew to fill a bowl, but leaving the surrounding ground dry. Just to be sure, Gideon asked God to let it be dry only on the fleece, with the ground covered with dew. God did so.

With the promise of God secured, Gideon proceeded to gather an army of thirty-two thousand men. But the Lord said to Gideon:

> "The people with you are too many for me to give the Midianites into their hand, lest Israel vaunt themselves against me, saying 'My own hand has delivered me.' Now therefore proclaim in the ears of the people, saying, 'Whoever is fearful and trembling, let him return home.'" (Jgs 7:2-3 RSV)

When Gideon tested them, only ten thousand remained.

But the Lord said there were still too many. He instructed Gideon to separate further the soldiers by taking only those men who drank water from the river by gathering it in their hands rather than lapping it up like dogs. Only three hundred men remained.

And the Lord said to Gideon, "With the three hundred men that lapped I will deliver you, and give the Midianites into your hand" (Jgs 7:7 RSV). The Lord delivered them just as he promised, even though the enemy "lay along the valley like locusts for multitude; and their camels were without number, as the sand which is upon the seashore for multitude" (Jgs 7:12 RSV).

What a remarkable demonstration of the power of God! Such is the strength available to us through the indwelling Comforter, who comes to help us to endure suffering. How can there be strength in weakness? Why is there power in trials? This seems to be a paradox.

By the world's standards, the Christian has nothing going for him. God deliberately chose what was weak and despised in the eyes of the world for a reason:

> For consider your call, brethren; not many of you were wise according to worldly standards, not many were powerful, not many were of noble birth. But God chose what is foolish in the world to shame the wise, God chose what is weak in the world to shame the strong. God chose what is low and despised in the world, even things that are not, to bring to nothing things that are, so that no human being might boast in the presence of God.
> (1 Cor 1:26-29 RSV)

God knows the weakness of our flesh. He knows we would easily boast in our own strength. But how can we boast in our weakness? God is pleased to send the Comforter to help us in our need, as long as we keep clearly in mind to whom the glory of victory and deliverance belongs.

Weakness is necessary to experience the grace of God. Through the recognition of our weakness and sin, we come to know our need for a Savior. We are in constant need of him, for without him we can do nothing. The trap of self-sufficiency quickly shuts off God's power, but God uses the broken and humble person to accomplish mighty deeds. Indeed, the times of most desperate need are most likely to call forth a plea from our hearts and lips: "Come, Holy Spirit."

Paul was surrounded by trials and knew his weakness. He was a man of flesh and blood who participated in murder by consenting to Stephen's death. We are told the story of his conversion in the ninth chapter of Acts:

> But Saul, still breathing threats and murder against the disciples of the Lord, went to the high priest and asked him for letters to the synagogues at Damascus, so that if he found any belonging to the Way, men or women, he might bring them bound to Jerusalem. (Acts 9:1-2 RSV)

Paul perceived himself as a man of power and influence. Within his own world, he surely was. But on this journey to Damascus, Paul was suddenly blinded by a light from heaven.

And he fell to the ground and heard a voice saying to him, "Saul, Saul, why do you persecute me?" And he said, "Who are you, Lord?" And he said, "I am Jesus whom you are persecuting; but rise and enter the city, and you will be told what you are to do."
(Acts 9:4-6 RSV)

Now that Paul had been made aware of his weakness, he was able to realize the saving power of God. Like a child, he was led by the hand into Damascus. "For three days, he was without sight, and neither ate nor drank" (Acts 9:9 RSV). Paul failed, he sinned, and he repented. God sent a disciple named Ananias to restore his sight.

The Lord comforted Ananias who was fearful of helping this dangerous persecutor of the Christians: "Go, for he is a chosen instrument of mine to carry my name before the Gentiles and kings and the sons of Israel; for I will show him how much he must suffer for the sake of my name" (Acts 9:15-16 RSV).

God imparted power to Paul to prepare him for his ministry. He received visions and revelations of the Lord, and wrote of even being "caught up into heaven" (2 Cor 12:2 RSV). Even though he experienced the Lord working so powerfully in his life, Paul says that he will not boast on his own behalf, except of his weaknesses. Indeed, the Lord had taught Paul this lesson in a very tangible way:

And to keep me from being too elated by the abundance of revelations, a thorn was given me in the flesh, a messenger of Satan, to harass me, to keep me from being too elated. Three times I besought the Lord about this, that it should leave me; but he said to me, "My grace is sufficient for you, for my power is made perfect in weakness."

I will all the more gladly boast of my weaknesses, that the power of Christ may rest upon me. For the sake of Christ, then, I am content with weaknesses, insults, hardships, persecutions, and calamities; for when I am weak, then I am strong.
(2 Cor 12:7-10 RSV)

There is the paradox. The power of God is perfected or brought to completion in our very weakness. The grace of God is sufficient to overcome our weakness. If we think we are strong, we are actually weak. If we realize we are weak, then we can receive the grace of God through the action of the Comforter to accomplish what he asks of us.

Jesus himself died in weakness and rose in power. The glory of the resurrection shines forth in us when we are deprived of the resources we think we need. What are those things that we think are so necessary to the abundant life—health, prosperity, popularity, approval, success, knowing important people, having influence?

People may say about us, "These people have nothing going for them. They're not too bright. They don't have any big contacts. They don't know how to dress. They really don't know anything. But when they speak, lives are changed. There must be something to what they say about this Jesus."

Such people fail to perceive the mystery: by God's intention, the church in this world is a suffering church, just as Christ was a suffering Christ. Our afflictions enable us to share in the sufferings of Christ and to receive the help of the Holy Spirit as Comforter. Then we in turn are able to offer comfort to others.

Listen to what Paul says in writing his Second Letter to the Corinthians:

Blessed be the God and Father of our Lord Jesus Christ, the Father of mercies and *God of all comfort*, who comforts us in all our affliction, with the comfort with which we ourselves are comforted by God. For as we share abundantly in Christ's sufferings, so through Christ we share abundantly in comfort too. (2 Cor 1:3-5 RSV)

Later, in the same letter, Paul says,

We are afflicted in every way, but not crushed; perplexed, but not driven to despair; persecuted, but not forsaken; struck down, but not destroyed; always carrying in the body the death of Jesus, so that the life of Jesus may also be manifested in our bodies. (2 Cor 4:8-10 RSV)

Our primary suffering should not stem from our own personal afflictions, however painful they may be. We are called to share the agony of Christ over the anguish of the world. When it is not mere sentimentality, the grief of the church over the state of the human race becomes prophetic light and power to bring the Word of God to a dying world. The Comforter longs to reveal the love of God to all those who suffer.

"DO NOT FEAR"

Fear is a good example of the kind of trial we all face in this world. What makes us afraid? Have you ever met anyone without fear? Well-trained athletes do not seem fearful, but in fact they often experience interior fear. Their egos don't want to lose to the competition. They can be especially afraid of injury or losing their health.

Have you ever met anyone who experiences real freedom from fear? Such a person's ego and flesh have been broken. He or she lives as a humble servant of God's plans. A clear conscience before God gives such people strength to go on in the face of difficulties. The work of the Comforter in their lives is very apparent.

Fear is more powerful when our expectation of help is dim. "For fear is nothing but surrender of the helps that come from reason; and the inner expectation of help, being weak, prefers ignorance of what causes the torment" (Wis 17:12-13 RSV). We are afraid of difficulties to the degree that we think there is no solution. If we do not think there is any way out, we are afraid really to look at the problem squarely. Our fear of death stems from this fact.

We can see this principle clearly demonstrated in people's lives. Have you ever had a friend whose business was undoubtedly headed for bankruptcy? We keep warning him, "Be careful! Sell out now or you're going to be in big trouble." But he replies, "Not me! I'm no quitter. I'm going to borrow a couple of hundred thousand from the bank and change my inventory. Things are going to be okay. You'll see." He cannot face failure, so he goes on denying the inevitable outcome.

Or consider the example of a woman whose marriage is in serious difficulty. Though her friends encourage her to seek help, she refuses. "We're just going through a little rough spot. Tom needs time to work things out on his own. He really doesn't mean to drink so much. We'll come out of this together. You'll see." Because she is surrounded by problems for which she sees no solution, she is full of fear and cannot face them.

The reason we are full of fear is that we are not willing to look at the source of the problems we face. *The source of our fear—the reason we crumble before obstacles—is our unrepented sin.* We are really in fear of God. Sin is the source of our difficulties. If we would look at the sin and experience the greatness of the salvation God offers to us, we would be free from fear. The Holy Spirit wants to convict us of our sin and help us to repent.

Many years ago, I was living in Jerusalem during a period of political unrest and violent rioting. Someone who was usually reliable had a spiritual sense that I was going to be shot and killed that year. I lived there one year in fear of my life.

Whenever I left my house, I wondered whether this would be the day when death would find me. I had to walk down streets with bullets whizzing by and rocks being hurled from the tops of buildings. I willed myself to keep going. "It's God's will that I am here," I told myself and everyone else who feared for my safety. I forced myself to go about my business—despite the fear I had and the violent situations I often witnessed.

Some years later, I was back in Jerusalem again, and a tourist had just been shot. Since the political situation was still much the same, the old fears welled up, along with my old ways of dealing with them. I gritted my teeth, toughened my mind, and willed myself to go on despite my fear.

But the Lord had another idea. "You mean well," he said to me, "but you are relying on your flesh. Submit your willpower and your flesh to me, and let me deal with it."

I did. All day long, I said the prayer, "Come, Holy Spirit." In fact, I repented of the fears that came from my flesh and asked the Lord to substitute them with his courage.

The Holy Spirit began to comfort and strengthen me. I experienced his power giving me a new authority over the fear. I completed my visit in total peace—the peace that flows from the Lord's merciful love, not a false peace that comes from willpower. I knew that the Holy Spirit himself was dealing with my fears, rather than leaving me to the resources of my own flesh.

The good news is that salvation begins now, not when we die.

Now we have a Savior. One of *us* is the Son of God. One of *us* is God. Jesus himself suffered the consequences of our sin to gain our freedom.

The Christians were exhorted in Peter's letter not to fear the unbelievers. He promised that those who suffer for the sake of righteousness will be blessed. What matters most is our zeal for the kingdom of God (1 Pt 3:13-15). In other words, if we are submitting to Jesus as our Lord, we will not be afraid. What harm can others do to us?

In exhorting these Christians not to be afraid of those who persecuted them, the author of First Peter was actually referring to a passage in Isaiah.

> For the Lord spoke thus to me with his strong hand upon me, and warned me not to walk in the way of this people, saying: "Do not call conspiracy all that this people call conspiracy, and do not fear what they fear, nor be in dread. But the Lord of hosts, him you shall regard as holy; let him be your fear, and let him be your dread. And he will become a sanctuary, and a stone of offense, and a rock of stumbling to both houses of Israel, a trap and a snare to the inhabitants of Jerusalem. And many shall stumble thereon; they shall fall and be broken; they shall be snared and taken." (Is 8:11-15 RSV)

Isaiah was given this advice about 730 B.C. The people of Israel were in danger of invasion. They were so worried about their safety that they were ready to make an alliance with anyone. Just like us, they were tempted to fall back on their own resources.

God was saying, "You cannot save yourself and this city on your own resources. Only in my power and by my will can you be saved. Do not be afraid of the things that are making everyone else afraid. Don't worry about these armies coming to attack you. They cannot really harm you. If you fear anything, fear the sin and infidelity in your heart and in the hearts of the people. That is what will do you harm."

Jesus expressed the same truth to his disciples:

> "I tell you, my friends, do not fear those who kill the body, and after that have no more that they can do. But I will warn you

whom to fear: fear him who, after he has killed, has power to cast into hell; yes, I tell you, fear him! Are not five sparrows sold for two pennies? And not one of them is forgotten before God. Why, even the hairs of your head are all numbered. Fear not; you are of more value than many sparrows."(Lk 12:4-7 RSV)

Freedom from fear is a deep inner work of the Holy Spirit as the Comforter. When the author of First Peter prepared Christians to suffer, he was appealing to their minds, not their emotions. Emotional preparation will not last. Conviction in the mind—the kind that no one can take away—is the only thing that will last.

Paul says that the kingdom of God is joy in the Holy Spirit (Rom 14:17). Such joy doesn't depend on our moods or circumstances. It is an abiding work of the Holy Spirit. This joy can certainly have a strong emotional content. But the joy to which Paul is referring is more permanent than the happiness produced by passing circumstances.

Read what Paul endured to bring salvation to people: shipwrecked a day and a night at sea, beaten, stoned and left for dead, imprisoned, betrayed by his old Jewish companions, betrayed by false Christians, he experienced danger on the road, many sleepless nights, frequent hunger and thirst, cold and exposure (2 Cor 11:23-28).

How was Paul able to endure these endless hardships? *Through faith.* He knew that God was able to sustain him and strengthen him in any circumstance. Paul was not afraid to face each new day.

Jesus taught about this reality in the last of the beatitudes:

"Blessed are those who are persecuted for righteousness' sake, for theirs is the kingdom of heaven. Blessed are you when men revile you and persecute you and utter all kinds of evil against you falsely on my account. Rejoice and be glad, for your reward is great in heaven." (Mt 5:10-12 RSV)

That is very difficult to do! No one enjoys being reviled, persecuted, and slandered. But if we suffer for the sake of Christ, we will come into our full inheritance. If we grasp and clutch the meager rewards this world offers, we risk losing the kingdom of heaven.

HEIRS OF THE KINGDOM

For those who are being led by the Spirit of God, these are the sons of God. For you did not receive a spirit of slavery, for fear again; but you received a Spirit of sonship in which we cry Abba, Father! The Spirit himself bears witness to our spirit that we are children of God. If children, then heirs as well: heirs of God and coheirs of Christ, if indeed we are "co-suffering" so that we will also be "co-glorified."(Rom 8:14-17)

God says, "I have already made out my will and testament, and listed you as my heirs. You will have everything that I have. You have eternal life. You are heirs of my kingdom."

We say, "That's wonderful! But can you give me a small guarantee that it's really true?" God says, "Guarantee? My Spirit lives in you. He is the down payment, the pledge of your inheritance. Any time you wonder if you are on the way to eternal life, stop and beg the Holy Spirit to reveal his love and power in you" (see Ephesians 1:13-14).

We have now within us that principle which will keep us alive for eternity. We live by the power of the Holy Spirit who is poured out in our hearts.

The Holy Spirit is ready to reveal the Father to us, to show us who the Father is. In this work, he can change our whole lives. Even in our poor, broken, sinful bodies, we can relate to God the way God always wanted us to. We can know him as Father.

As sons and daughters of God, we can call out, "Abba, Father." Did you know that this means "Dad"? Jesus himself always used this name for God, which must have shocked people. Every time he spoke of God, he said "Abba"—"my Dad." Especially in the depths of his suffering, he cried out, "Abba, Father, all things are possible to you; take this cup away from me; but not what I will but what you will" (Mk 14:36).

Knowing that the Holy Spirit of God dwells within us and that we are on the way to eternal life completely changes our perspective. What a great comfort and protection! We don't have to hang on fearfully to material possessions, reputation, or status. The pagans look after those things, Jesus said. But we have a Father in heaven who promises to provide all of our needs.

"Do not seek what you are to eat and what you are to drink, nor be of anxious mind. For all the nations of the world seek these things; and your Father knows that you need them. Instead, seek his kingdom, and these things shall be yours as well.

"Fear not, little flock, for it is your Father's good pleasure to give you the kingdom. Sell your possessions, and give alms; provide yourselves with purses that do not grow old, with a treasure in the heavens that does not fail, where no thief approaches and no moth destroys. For where your treasure is, there will your heart be also." (Lk 12:29-34 RSV)

Abraham demonstrated this kind of trust in God. God told Abraham, "Do you see this land? It's all yours. I am God. I own everything, and I give it to you." Abraham believed God. So when the servants of Lot and Abraham were having a problem sharing the land, Abraham was fearless. He said to Lot, "The whole land is before you. You go to the right, I'll go to the left. Or if you choose left, I'll go right" (see Genesis 13:9). Abraham knew that he didn't have to worry. God had given him the land. In his selfish desire for the lush green grass to feed his flocks, Lot chose the direction of Sodom and Gomorrah.

We do not need, like Lot, to continually look out for ourselves. Jesus tells us explicitly,

"What father among you, if his son asks for a fish, will instead of a fish give him a serpent; or if he asks for an egg, will give him a scorpion? If you then, who are evil, know how to give good gifts to your children, how much more will the heavenly Father give the Holy Spirit to those who ask him!"(Lk 11:11-13 RSV)

What is the best gift? The Holy Spirit, the giver of life itself, our Comforter and Counselor in trial and difficulty.

Because we are sons and daughters of God, we have the right to enter into God's presence, to present our needs before the Father. We have access to God. "Let us approach, then, with assurance the throne of grace that we might receive mercy and find grace at the right time of need" (Heb 4:16). Does that mean we're going to be with God sometime later? No, it means right now. When we pray, we know we're talking with someone who is listening and will answer.

Sometimes when we experience weakness, we want to hide from God and other people. Because of pride, we don't want to expose our weakness. Don't we realize how foolish that really is? If a good mother has a child that was born with severe physical defects, she loves the child nonetheless. In fact, the needier the child, the more likely the mother is to show tender love and care.

How can we fear God who died in weakness on our behalf? God knows our weakness even better than we do ourselves. He knows our every need before we even speak of it. The person who is truly humble before God will have the most confidence in God. Christians who know their own weakness will not trust themselves, but rather throw themselves on the mercy of their heavenly Father. They can say with Paul, "I can do all things in him who strengthens me" (Phil 4:13 RSV).

Where do we experience the greatest need in our lives? Our day-to-day existence can sometimes be fairly peaceful. But hidden from view are spiritual powers of darkness bent on our destruction. We are most in need of rescue from what we cannot even see.

EIGHT

God Rescues Us
from Evil

THERE WAS ONLY DARKNESS. The blindfold over my eyes completely blocked out the light. I was lying on my back on a low bed. The unforgettable sound of adhesive tape being unwound from its roll filled the room. Strong hands wrapped this wide packing tape around my head, over my forehead, eyes, and mouth, and around my neck. Only a small space over my nostrils was left open.

Next, my arms and hands were held close to my sides, and the tape was wound slowly around my whole body, starting with the legs and moving up past my shoulders. I was being totally encased. Someone forced me into a sitting position, and another layer of tape was wound around my neck, under my chin, and over the top of my head. I was a hostage bound.

Arms lifted me from the bed and carried me out. My body was pushed into a long narrow container. I heard the lid being closed and bolted over me. I could feel solid metal through my shoeless feet. I raised my head a few inches and struck a solid metal top. I moved my hips from side to side as best I could and found metal on either side. I lay there like a corpse in a coffin.

I heard an engine start, gears grind, and a metal door open. Only when it lurched forward did I realize I was on a truck. To add to my terror, I could now smell heavy exhaust fumes coming up through the floor of the truck body. I must be right over the tailpipe. Already I was breathing heavily through my nose.

God, I prayed, *don't let the air passages clog!*

This harrowing experience is retold by Benjamin Weir, a Presbyterian minister seized on the streets of Beirut in May of 1984 by a group of Shiite Muslim extremists *(Hostage Bound, Hostage Free* by Ben and Carol Weir, The Westminster Press, Philadelphia, 1987, p. 9). The painful ordeal of his sixteen months' imprisonment is filled with the faithfulness of God.

Reverend Weir nourished his faith by praying and dwelling on hymns and Scripture passages. Thinking at one point that he was being taken out for execution, he prayed: *"Lord, give me faith now to trust you. I am yours and in your hands. Whether in life or death, help me to know I belong to you"* (*ibid.,* p. 89). He repeated the Twenty-Third Psalm and was immediately encouraged by the promise of God: "Even though I walk through the valley of the shadow of death, I fear no evil; for thou art with me; thy rod and thy staff, they comfort me" (Ps 23:4 RSV).

God sent the Holy Spirit to comfort Reverend Ben Weir. Finally, after fourteen months, he was allowed to talk with Father Martin Jenco, a Roman Catholic priest who had been taken hostage eight months after Reverend Weir. They took turns leading daily worship services with a few other hostages, and one of them would save a piece of bread from the morning meal for Communion. Father Jenco referred to this as "Jesus being nearby," an invaluable source of strength and nourishment.

Meanwhile Carol Weir doggedly worked through official channels to secure her husband's release. His four children agonized over what might be happening to their father. His family, friends, and many church members prayed fervently for Ben's safety.

Two months after the kidnapping, his family saw his pale and bearded face on a videotaped statement urging the release of seventeen political prisoners in Kuwait. They had to wait fourteen more months to see Ben in person. Reverend Ben Weir was finally set free in September of 1985 to convey a message to the United States government.

Almost a year later, he was reunited with Father Jenco, who had just been released five days earlier. They embraced as brothers in the Lord, tearfully and joyously, deeply thankful that God had delivered them both from captivity.

God has delivered us from something even greater than the captivity of these hostages: spiritual bondage to this present evil age. Not only has he sent us a comforter in our hour of trial, God has also delivered us from a *spiritual terrorism* that holds our worldly systems in captivity.

Our human condition outside of the light of Christ is pitiable. We dwell in darkness and gloom, each of us imprisoned in one way or another. Having rebelled against God's truth, we fall down under the weight of our burdens. There is no one who can deliver us.

> They dwelt in darkness and in gloom,
> bondsmen in want and in chains,
> because they had rebelled against the words of God,
> and scorned the counsel of the Most High.
> And he humbled their hearts with trouble;
> when they stumbled, there was no one to help them.
> They cried to the Lord in their distress;
> from their straits he rescued them.
> And he led them forth from darkness and gloom,
> and broke their bonds asunder.
> Let them give thanks to the Lord for his kindness,
> and for his wondrous deeds to the children of men,
> For he shattered the gates of brass,
> and burst the bars of iron. (Ps 107:10-16)

When we cry out to the Lord, he rescues us. His power is far greater than gates of brass or bars of iron. Let us give thanks to God for his steadfast love and mercy!

Sometimes, however, we don't even recognize the chains which hold us captive. Invisible bonds of fear, loneliness, and despair can hold us more tightly than brass and iron. Yet we can fail to see our need for deliverance.

We cannot perceive the depth of our darkness except in the light of redemption. Without a living experience of the reality and majesty of Jesus Christ, it is impossible to comprehend our captivity. For "the god of this world has blinded the minds of the unbelievers, to keep them from seeing the light of the gospel of the glory of Christ, who is the likeness of God" (2 Cor 4:4 RSV).

Yet God is able to bring forth new life in the midst of utter darkness. "The God who said, 'Let light shine out of darkness,' has shone in our hearts" (2 Cor 4:6a RSV). By the grace of God, we receive "the light of the knowledge of the glory of God in the face of Christ" (2 Cor 4:6b RSV).

Our new life in Christ is just as real as the world in which we live. But do we see the world as it really is? Do we accurately perceive the forces of darkness that are at work around us? Indeed, those same forces are also at work in us, and will kill us unless we are purified by the blood of Christ. This is serious business.

THE DOMINION OF DARKNESS

> Grace to you and peace from God our Father and the Lord Jesus Christ, who gave himself for our sins that he might rescue us from the *present evil age* according to the will of our God and Father; to whom be glory for ages and ages. Amen. (Gal 1:3-5)

What is this "present evil age"? It is the very world that we live in. Especially as the vision and influence of Christianity diminish, we can see more and more clearly the dominion of darkness.

Often, the ugliness of sin stops masquerading under the guise of respectability and rages fullblown in the destruction of lives. The rampages of violence that characterize some international soccer games or local rock concerts come from pent-up rage and frustration. What causes this?

When teenagers decide to have fun by going "wilding" in Central Park, and mercilessly beat and rape a woman almost to death—where does this come from? Experts blame everything from physiological abnormalities to movies, rock music, and television shows which glorify brutality.

In your own life, when somebody cuts you off in traffic and you go crazy, what's wrong? Where does that anger and rage come from?

These are symptoms of the present evil age. Our lives are out of control. Some things are only annoying, like hikes in the price of gasoline. Some are difficult, like paying taxes. And some are downright oppressive, like the fact that you can't turn on the television without being bombarded by sex, violence, and the endless pursuit of pleasure.

Most people walk around incredibly frustrated and angry and unable to face it. That's why there is so much alcoholism and addiction to drugs, so much depression and meaninglessness. People are trying to cope with a bondage that ends in death.

The fear of death is the source of our bondage. In American society, we don't know how to handle it when a friend's mom or dad dies. We avoid the bereaved person and don't know how to express our condolences. If we bump into the bereaved, we apologetically mumble some trite phrase and leave in awkward and confused silence. We try to shield children especially from the reality of death. If at all possible, dying family members are removed to the sanitary and safe confines of a hospital.

We are afraid of anything that diminishes who we are. Any slight foretaste of death, any intimation of our fragile nature, any reminder of the short and narrow confines of our existence—all these things frighten us. Rather than face them, we sell out to values that corrupt our lives. Thus, we are in bondage.

Jesus knows our captivity.

> Since, then, the children share blood and flesh, he too likewise partook with them so that through death he might render impotent him who held the power of death, that is, the devil, and free those who through fear of death throughout all their life were held in slavery. (Heb 2:14-15)

Madison Avenue also knows us well. Most advertising firms have a staff of psychiatrists and psychologists to manipulate this fear of death. Usually the message is quite subtle. Drinking Michelob beer promises power over the night, happiness, and a beautiful blonde. Buying a Chrysler Le Baron guarantees "crystal key" care along with power and prestige. Taking Excedrin offers more effective relief from headaches "this big." These ads imperceptibly promise to delay the inevitability of diminishment and death.

But deep down inside, we know that our struggle against death is a losing battle. We can become angry, frustrated, and confused. Life in this present evil age is a bondage.

One of the worst forms of bondage we face in this age of hedonism and selfish pursuits is meaninglessness, especially among our young people. This total loss of meaning has given rise to a rash of teenage suicides. Despair is very characteristic of our age, and is not confined to people caught in poverty.

I live in an upper-middle class neighborhood. One day, I saw a bumper sticker on the back of a car which read, *"The one who dies with the most toys wins."* Doesn't such wittiness reflect deep anger, despair, and rebellion against God? The message is that life is meaningless. Sure! Get a hot tub, a Mercedes, and a condominium in Florida, but so what? Even though you win—because you have all those toys—you still die.

How can you have won when you no longer exist? Where is the consolation in a childish pursuit of material possessions whose value exists only as long as the game is played? There is none, because we all lose this game at the buzzer. Yet our consumer society is built around such empty values. No one wants to face this truth for fear of seeing the hollowness he or she has embraced as the very reason for living.

I recently served on a retreat for a group of very intelligent, successful people in the Washington, D.C., area; young professionals making huge salaries. I spoke to them about being saved from this present evil age. When some of them came to talk to me, they said, "You know, my life is out of control. I've got to pay for my Jacuzzi and my Porsche. I have expensive condominium payments. I've got to keep up. I'm already behind everybody else. I know I eat too much, drink too much, smoke too much. My sex life is out of order. I've lost control of my own life. What can I do?"

These people were at least able to articulate the bondage of this present evil age. So I said to them, "Why don't you get out of it?" Some of them were truly frightened by the prospect. "I can't get out of it. I don't want to get out of it. Look at what I'll have to give up—my condominium, my Jacuzzi, my Porsche. I'll have to get an apartment. Without my Jacuzzi, I'll have to take a shower like everybody else. And drive a Chevrolet instead of a Porsche! Even worse, what will my peers think? If I don't keep up with the competition, I'll be ridiculed as a failure."

These were good, Catholic folks on a retreat. They could have done a lot of things that weekend. I'm talking about earnest seekers of God. These people were frightened at the prospect of changing their lifestyle.

Does this sound far-fetched? Unfortunately, being caught in the rat race or keeping up with the in-crowd dominates most of the upper-middle class people in our society. And what dominates those middle-class and below is the desire to accumulate the so-called "good things of life." They want to get what they're missing and make up for lost time.

I spoke to the people at the retreat about praying, about turning their lives over to Jesus. We prayed together. I taught them what it means to give their lives every day to the power of the cross.

Some of them accepted the grace that the Lord was offering and did get out of the trap they were in. I don't mean these young people stopped working for a living. Rather, they got out of the rat race and out of the bondage by asserting their freedom as Christians. They let the Lord change their minds and give them a new vision of reality. Now when I see them, their lives are different, their faces are different.

As we have seen, a life of bondage does not include only people at the bottom of the economic ladder. Many powerful executives at the top have often lost all meaning to their lives. Meaning is that backdrop against which we can put our experiences and make sense out of them.

If we don't have a vision for our life, then our life makes no sense. Something besides sheer accumulation of power or money or possessions has to bring cohesion, order, and understanding to our experiences. If not, we can be great successes in the business world and be alcoholics. Or else, we can have a family and still have our whole sexual life out of order.

What are some of the symptoms of meaninglessness? Anger, greed, brittle relationships, despair, immorality, confusion especially in the area of sexuality—just to name a few. These are part of the price we pay for our rebellion.

And as they did not see fit to recognize God, God gave them over to an unfit mind, to do that which is wrong: filled with every kind of injustice, wickedness, greed, malice; full of envy, murder, strife, deceit, malignity; gossips, slanderers, inimical to God, insolent, arrogant, boastful, inventors of evil, rebellious to parents, without understanding, without loyalty, without natural affection, without mercy. These, knowing well the just decree of God, that those who practice these things are worthy of death, not only do them, but even approve others who practice them. (Rom 1:28-32)

The price we pay for the luxury of rebellion is far too great! Thanks be to God, "who has delivered us from this dominion of darkness and transferred us to the kingdom of his beloved Son, in whom we have redemption, the forgiveness of sins" (Col 1:13-14 RSV).

God has saved us from this present evil age. His solution to the weakness of the human frame is grace. Our redemption from darkness, despair, and death is the work of God.

What does it mean to be saved? *Our salvation in Christ should be just as perceptible as our bondage to this evil age without Christ.* Faith is not given only to promise happiness in the hereafter—while permitting confusion and bondage to sin here on earth. That wouldn't make any sense.

Paul wrote to the Galatians about this deception:

O senseless Galatians, who has bewitched you before whose eyes Jesus Christ was portrayed crucified! I want to learn only this from you: was it from works of the law that you received the Spirit or from the message of faith? Are you so senseless? Having begun in the Spirit, do you now end in the flesh? Did you experience such things in vain? (Gal 3:1-4)

Paul is appealing to the spiritual experience of the Galatians. His whole argument depends upon the fact that they once lived in darkness, but now they know light. They were once at point A, but have been moved to point B. He asks them to reflect: did their experience of the Holy Spirit come from "works of the law" or "hearing with faith"?

Paul is reminding the Galatians that freedom from spiritual bondage cannot be achieved by our own striving. We're not playing a game of make-believe, while we wait to receive the reality of heaven. The death of Jesus Christ actually makes the freedom *from* this present evil age as real as the bondage *in* this present evil age. We ought to know we are free.

How do we enter into this freedom? Very simply. We turn our lives over to Jesus Christ and repent of our sin. We tell the Lord we don't want sin in our lives anymore. We cannot be free of this present evil age on our own. The message of salvation is good news because God accomplishes this work of grace in us.

SATAN HATES GOD

Now we come to one of the most important works of the Holy Spirit. The Holy Spirit gives us strength and wisdom in our conflict with the world and with spiritual powers. Behind the evils of the world is an organized complicity that resists the truth at all times. And behind that resistance rests a power—a spiritual personality who hates God. Our conflict rests basically with him.

We have to be realistic. Satan hates God. And he hates us because God loves us so much. By destroying us, he can get at God. A ruined life, a broken body, a broken mind, a damned soul—these are nothing to Satan as long as he can ruin God's work.

Terrorism exemplifies the way Satan and the systems of this world join together to seek our destruction. Sometimes individuals are subjected to cruel kidnapping. Other extremists seize airliners or cruise ships and threaten to destroy the lives of all on board. Terrorists have no respect for human life.

Ignatius of Loyola called Satan "the enemy of mankind." Emotional problems, broken homes, sickness, or poverty are simply ways to ruin the image of God in humanity. But the worst assault is eternal damnation—to separate people from God forever.

But doesn't God control the world? Of course, God is ultimately in control. Nothing happens without his permission. The physical world is God's creation over which he rules. Yet there is a worldly system which Satan controls. "The whole world is in the power of the evil one" (1 Jn 5:19 RSV).

Because of a rebellion against our Creator, we have constructed a whole complex system of sin in which we ourselves participate. I have already referred to this as the "structures of sin." This system finds expression in the political, emotional, economic, cultural, mental, and demonic forces that rule the world.

All of this is encouraged and used by the evil one for his own purposes. As people give in more and more to the world and its demands, Satan manipulates them. They fall into greater bondage as Satan cultivates the illusion of darkness.

That is why we are told to be prepared for battle:

> Finally, be strengthened in the Lord and in the might of his power. Take on the whole battle equipment of God so that you are able to stand against the schemes of the devil. For our struggle is not against blood and flesh but against principalities, against powers, against the world-rulers of this darkness, against the spirit-forces of wickedness in the heavenly realm. For this reason, take up the whole battle equipment of God so that you might be able to withstand them on the evil day, and having accomplished everything, to stand. (Eph 6:10-13)

Satan is the ruler of this world. Do we recognize the hold that he has upon us? Or are we too busy fighting with our husbands, wives, children, parents, friends, or co-workers? Have we put on God's armor, or are we too busy fighting in our own strength?

Satan is very clever. We can get so caught up in fighting each other and pouring all our energy into the problems of this world that we miss the real battle. Our conflict is ultimately not with the people with whom we live and work. Our real struggle is with the spiritual powers that bring about these problems.

Some people say, "But I don't believe in the devil." If we take our Christian commitment seriously, the devil is going to be right there. We're going to have to fight with him, whether we like it or not. If we begin a spiritual life in earnest, we'll find out soon enough that Satan does exist.

Put on the whole armor of God that you may be able to stand your ground. What is the armor of God?

> Stand then, your bodies belted round with truth, and wearing the breastplate of righteousness, and feet shod in readiness [to preach] the Good News of peace; take up with all these, the shield of faith with which you will be able to put out all the flaming darts of the evil one; and take up the helmet of salvation, and the sword of the Spirit, which is the word of God; with all prayer and supplication. (Eph 6:14-18)

Practically speaking, Paul exhorts us to stand firm in our faith, to be on guard, not to fall asleep. The truth of God needs to fill our minds. We need to be careful to live righteously so that Satan does not gain a foothold in our hearts because of sin. As we are concerned and active in serving the needs of others and spreading God's love and mercy, we are less vulnerable to self-pity and pride. Faith is the shield that protects our hearts from Satan's fiery darts. The knowledge of our salvation is the helmet that protects our minds from doubt and fear.

Christians need not only to be vigilant against attack, but to go on the offensive against Satan as well. The sword of the Spirit is a powerful offensive weapon against the forces of darkness. Many Christians have decided actively to speak out and fight against evils such as abortion or the practice of homosexuality.

Finally, we are exhorted to spend time in prayer. Praying in the Spirit keeps us attuned to God, and calls forth the power of God in our battle against the powers of darkness. Rather than rest in our own salvation, we need to be on our knees for the sake of the world.

The Holy Spirit will strengthen us in our fight against the hosts of wickedness. The Lord promises to protect those whom he has chosen to do his will.

THE WORLD IS WRONG

When we stand in the truth, we will meet with opposition. But the Lord tells us over and over again, "Do not be afraid. You're not alone. You're not doing this on your own power. The worst that can happen to you is that you'll die. If they kill you for my sake, then you'll be blessed. Do not be afraid. I will be with you."

We are in bondage to this present evil age because we fear other people more than we fear God. But the Lord has promised to prove the world wrong:

> And when he comes, he will prove the world wrong concerning sin and justice and judgment: concerning sin, because they do not believe in me; concerning justice, because I go to the Father, and you will see me no more; concerning judgment, because the ruler of this world has been judged. (Jn 16:8-11)

To whom will the Holy Spirit prove the world wrong? To the followers of Christ. If the world were to accept that it is wrong, it would cease to be the world and become the kingdom of God. This text is speaking about the testimony of the Holy Spirit to believers.

This world is wrong about sin because people don't believe in Jesus. That is the crux of our sin. We need conversion from the heart and forgiveness of sins. We don't need more solutions to the problems of poverty, mental health, and disease that rely exclusively on human resources. We need Jesus.

Those in the church are wrong whenever they opt for solutions that aren't primarily based on salvation through Christ. Some forms of liberation theology provide a good example. While justifiably concerned with the burning issue of poverty, some Latin American priests have tended to make Christianity into a political Marxist doctrine to counter injustice. Salvation cannot be equated with such political and social liberation.

We are called to transform the world—to be *in* the world, but not *of* it. The church is called to perform a particular function in the world today:

> The Church maintains that beneath all that changes there is much that is unchanging, much that has its ultimate foundation in Christ, who is the same yesterday, and today, and forever. And that is why the Council, relying on the inspiration of Christ, the image of the invisible God, the firstborn of all creation, proposes to speak to all men in order to unfold the mystery that is man and cooperate in tackling the main problems facing the world today. (*Vatican II: Gaudium et Spes,* #10)

We in the church are encouraged to enter into meaningful dialogue about current pressing world problems such as eradicating the threat of nuclear weapons or helping the poor. Our primary commitment must be to Christ, and our political and social efforts must flow from that commitment.

A false tension has been set up between social action and the gospel. Fortunately, we see the gospel clearly and dramatically demonstrated in the work of Mother Teresa of Calcutta. The Missionaries of Charity nurse the sick and the dying destitutes, gather and teach street children, visit and care for beggars and leprosy patients, give shelter to the abandoned and homeless. They deliver the message of the love of Christ to the poorest of the poor.

I attended a conference recently where a girl received a healing word of knowledge. Having been rejected by her family, she heard God say to her that he was her family. A vision of the Blessed Virgin convinced her that she had a spiritual mother tenderly watching over her.

All of the social agencies in the world could not have done for that girl what Jesus Christ and his mother did for her that night. Jesus cared for a girl that was thrown out by her own family. He died for her and he wants her to know his love so that she will live with him forever. God rescued her from this present darkness.

The world is wrong concerning justice because it doesn't recognize Jesus as the Just One. What is the world's idea of Jesus? "A nice guy. He really tried hard, but he had some ideas that were totally unrealistic. He thought somehow the kingdom of God was going to come in. He even had this idea that if he went to Jerusalem and died, then he could hasten its coming. So, he died. That was very sad."

We know that Jesus Christ is alive. Jesus did usher in the kingdom of God. There is no *justice* apart from the blood of Jesus Christ (Rom 3:25). The word *justice* also means *vindication*. God raised Jesus from the dead to vindicate his obedience unto death.

The world is wrong concerning judgment because the prince of this world has already been judged. The one who rules this world has already been condemned. We cannot look to this world to dictate how we are to live. People think they know what makes he world go round, but they don't. The Lord says, "I make the world go round. Nothing happens that is not subject to my authority. People are not going to decide when the world ends. I am. People are not going to decide the way things are to go. I am."

One of the deepest sins in our hearts is cynical unbelief. Often we don't really believe that God is serious about his promises to us. We think, "God doesn't really pay much attention to me. Things are not going to get much better. The sin I'm in, I'll always be in. I'll go to confession, and hope I die in the state of grace. The mess the world is in will never change either. Let's be realistic. Messed-up people give birth to messed-up people. That's the way the world goes."

What are we really saying? "There is no power in this world except what we can see. We can pray for a little while and feel better, but nothing is really going to change." If we fear somewhere deep down that may turn out to be the case, then what happens? We surrender to the prince of this world, at least to some extent. Taken to its logical conclusion, that kind of cynical attitude condemns humanity to eternal death.

The truth is simply proclaimed in the Gospel of John:

For God loved the world so that he gave his only begotten Son, so that everyone believing in him may not perish, but may have eternal life. For God did not send the Son into the world that he might judge the world, but that the world might be saved through him. The one believing in him is not judged, the one not believing is already judged because he has not believed in the name of the only begotten Son of God.

This is the judgment: the light has come into the world and men loved the darkness rather than the light for their works were evil. For everyone carrying out evil hates the light, and does not come to the light, so that his works be not exposed. The one doing the truth comes to the light so that his works be manifest because they have been done in God. (Jn 3:16-21)

Jesus says, "Listen, the world is wrong about judgment. The Holy Spirit can prove it to you, first by changing your life so that you know the power of God." Power in this world to change, to bring people to eternal life, to transform people's minds—that power comes from the Son of God. That same power raised Jesus from the dead.

We believers have to be convinced that the world is wrong because we, too, live in the world. Jesus prayed not that we would be taken out of the world, but that we would be kept from the evil one:

> "They are not of the world, even as I am not of the world. Sanctify them in the truth; your word is truth. As you didst send me into the world, so I have sent them into the world. And for their sake I consecrate myself, that they also may be consecrated in truth." (Jn 17:16-19 RSV)

Even though we are not of the world, sometimes we give in to the evil one and invite part of the world to make a home in us. The Holy Spirit will prove that the worldly part of us is wrong. Then we will be free as believers to stand on the truth of God.

Salvation requires a change in our behavior and values. If we want to be free from sin—from anger, fear, compulsions and addictions—then we can't continue to expose ourselves to all the places where those spiritual powers have dominion. That means breaking with our old way of life—"no longer walking the way the pagans walk" (Eph 4:17).

When people become Christians in certain cultures—like Israel or India—they radically break away from their past. Often their family throws them out; perhaps they lose their jobs. They quit the whole way of life they had before, because they see where it is dominated by sin and darkness. They know that someone cannot become half a Christian, someone, for instance, who goes to church and still goes to see the witch doctor, or strives to find fulfillment solely in this life.

It is no different in our culture, which is essentially pagan. Many values in our minds, attitudes which have been bred into us, emotional reactions we have—all these are of darkness. We have to quit these ways and enter into the new life of Jesus. Our devotion to holiness should set us apart from the ways of the world.

The Spirit of the living God dwells within us. Jesus Christ is the only one who has the power to rescue us from this present evil age. "Little children, you are of God, and have overcome them; for he who is in you is greater than he who is in the world" (1 Jn 4:4 RSV).

Jesus wants to empower us by the Holy Spirit to live lives of holiness, right in the midst of this present darkness. Without the power of God, how can we hope to love one another, to serve one another, to proclaim the good news? How else can we learn truly to live again?

NINE

Empowered by the Holy Spirit

S USAN HAD BEEN RAISED AS A SOUTHERN BAPTIST. A strong conversion experience in an independent evangelical church
fueled her fundamentalist fervor. Susan's usual approach to
Catholics was to evangelize them—to convince them of salvation
by faith and not by works.

A few years later, Susan was baptized in the Holy Spirit and
became involved in an ecumenical, charismatic Christian community. After diligently shopping around for a local church, she
was disappointed to discover that all of them had drawbacks.

When Phil expressed interest in her, Susan's response was
simple: "I'm not planning to get involved with a Catholic!" But the
Lord had other plans. She and Phil began a relationship that
seemed to be heading toward marriage.

Thankfully, Phil did not put any pressure on Susan to become a
Catholic. In an effort to be open to the Lord, she attended an
instruction course. One presentation upset her so much that
Susan promptly walked out the door. Since her objections to
Catholic teaching seemed impossible to overcome, she resolved to
make the best of the situation.

Shortly before their wedding, Susan was reading a book about
marriage. Out of the blue, God showed her that she had fenced off
this area out of sheer independence—or stubborn self-will. If
Susan was going to come under the headship of Phil in marriage,

then in her case, God wanted her to submit this part of her life as well. Even though she meant well, Susan could see that she wasn't holding on to any strong faith tradition of her own. It was just that no church was good enough for an independent-minded perfectionist!

In response to the clear leading of the Lord, Susan was received into the Catholic church three days before her wedding. Even though she still had a multitude of unanswered questions, she knew this was God's intention for her. Susan has never been sorry for that decision, but amazed at the wonderful fruit it has borne in her life and in her family.

Susan's story reflects a common condition among God's people—deep-seated prejudice, fear and suspicion, doubt and criticism. Satan's strategy in this present evil age is simple. "Divide and conquer." Sow seeds of confusion, doubt, and darkness in the minds of men, women, even children. Add fuel to the fires of rebellion and self-will.

He has been pretty successful. Look at the broken condition of the world. Look at the deep divisions even within the body of Christ. Circumstantial evidence might suggest that Satan is winning the battle. Has God been caught napping, or perhaps been outmaneuvered?

Certainly not. God has the human situation in hand. The deep-rooted sin within us has resulted in divisions. Christians have suffered from the work of spiritual forces of darkness in the world. But God intends to rescue his people, and to set them as a shining light on a hill to vanquish the darkness.

Rather than isolate us, our differences were created by God so that we would recognize our need for one another. No one has all that he or she requires. Because we need each other, we can be even more deeply united. Together, we can be empowered to love and serve in a dying world.

Such is God's plan in building the body of Christ. There is "one Body and one Spirit, just as you were called in one hope of your calling; one Lord, one faith, one baptism, one God and Father of all, who is over all and through all and in all" (Eph 4:4-6).

The body of Christ is the masterpiece of God's work. By the power of the Holy Spirit, we are joined together even more deeply than a man and woman in marriage. Our unity flows from the fact that the Word of God became flesh. The fullness of the incarnation is available to us because Jesus died for us, rose for us, and poured out the Holy Spirit.

God wants to heal the isolation, the individualism, the competition, the suspicion, and the fear that divide us from one another. The Holy Spirit wants to restore our relationships and enable us to love one another.

It is important to realize the intimate connection between the unity of the body of Christ and the deep work of redemption that God wants to bring about in each of us. Rivalry, dissensions, factions, and jealousy will not inherit the kingdom of God (Gal 5:19-21). These are works of the flesh.

Many of the differences between church bodies of today are the continuation of an age-old tragedy. In the Old Testament, ten of the tribes of Israel broke away and rebelled against Solomon's son by forming the Northern Kingdom. This division further weakened the people of Israel, which made them more susceptible to attack from both within and without.

Just so, serious divisions were disrupting the Corinthian church. They were quarreling among themselves as to whom their allegiance belonged. Some proclaimed, "I belong to Paul," while others said "I belong to Apollos" or "I belong to Cephas" or "I belong to Christ." Each group thought it was entirely justified in its position.

Paul exhorted them:

> I appeal to you, brethren, by the name of our Lord Jesus Christ, that all of you agree and that there be no dissensions among you, but that you be united in the same mind and the same judgment. . . . Is Christ divided? Was Paul crucified for you? Or were you baptized in the name of Paul? (1 Cor 1:10-13 RSV)

Paul was asking them to take seriously the fact that all of them together formed Christ in this world. How many Christs are there? How can we divide ourselves into rival factions? What have we done to the mystery of the body of Christ? Divisions arise because of fleshly thinking about divine realities.

Paul proclaims that the healing for these divisions is "the Word of the Cross" (1 Cor 1:18). The body of Christ is formed when the

Holy Spirit joins us just as we are—weak and sinful human beings—to the risen Jesus. God himself wants to create this body as the normal place to bring about revelation—a place of power and transformation.

The solution to what is wrong with the whole body of Christ is the outpouring of the Holy Spirit. God is at work to restore us once again to a unity that has been fractured and ruined by our sin. Unity cannot be negotiated. We can't have unity by our own resources or by being nice people. Unity is achieved only by dying to our sins and living to God, having our spirits and minds renewed to understand God's plan of redemption.

We know the power of God at work in us to the degree that sin is being put to death and our minds are rejoicing in the reality and majesty of Jesus Christ. Then the power of God is poured out among us that we might love one another.

THE UNITY OF LOVE

Love is the glue that holds us all together. The Spirit's presence within us manifests itself as fruit, just as the life energy of a tree or plant produces fruit. You can't squeeze a piece of fruit out of yourself by sheer effort. Love is a fruit of the Holy Spirit. It takes time to grow.

"Having purified your souls by your obedience to the truth for a sincere love of the brethren, love one another earnestly from the heart" (1 Pt 1:22 RSV). Now that you are made pure because you have obeyed the truth, now you can love one another. That "love" is *anupokritos*—sincere love from the heart, love which is not hypocritical. This love has to come from a heart that is broken, a heart that seeks the good of another above oneself.

What is a broken heart? It is a heart that knows sin—how wily we are—and that knows redemption. Let us beg the Holy Spirit to heal and protect us from the deceit and wiliness of our minds—from the ways in which we avoid being obedient to the truth.

When we relate to people, is there a hidden agenda for our egos, our protection, our security, our advancement, or our own comfort? Or do we have sincere love?

Love is patient and kind; love is not jealous or boastful; it is not arrogant or rude. Love does not insist on its own way; it is not irritable or resentful; it does not rejoice at wrong, but rejoices in the right. Love bears all things, believes all things, hopes all things, endures all things. (1 Cor 13:4-8 RSV)

There is nothing more important than love. Sincere love comes from a heart in which the work of Jesus Christ has really taken place. Then we can honestly care about our brothers and sisters in Christ. We can honestly care about their salvation, and not be put off by our own need for approval. We will be able to speak the truth in love.

The unity of love is what the church is all about. Our love for one another cannot be founded on good feelings. "Warm fuzzies" are easily frosted. A married couple needs to learn how to communicate and serve one another after the honeymoon is over. We need to express committed love to our brothers and sisters in Christ who may appear less lovable in our own eyes.

The work of redemption is not all individual. This is the whole understanding of *church*: we need the sacraments, we need guidance, we need each other. We need the help of our brothers and sisters in Christ to grow the fruit of righteousness. Our commitment is to help one another work out our salvation. God works through our brothers and sisters to break our flesh and free us from the bondage of sin so that we can truly love one another. We see the effects of sin especially in our relationships.

Consider the example of a family on vacation. The husband is exhausted from long months of commuting and working. He's looking forward to two weeks of fishing and reading. His wife is looking forward to having him around to spend time with their young children. After the first week, his wife's forbearance begins to wear thin. Her husband's fishing and reading has only increased her burden. When they talk more about their individual needs, the husband decides to die to his selfish desires so that he can serve his wife. The family grows in unity through this experience.

We have to work at our relationships. They do not come easily in marriage or in the body of Christ. I have never heard of a family that was naturally harmonious and peaceful all the time. Differences of opinion abound about where to go for vacation, priorities for major purchases, when to go to church—any of the myriad details of daily life.

Our flesh does not want relationships based on sincere love. Too much pain and sacrifice are involved. Because the flesh is still with us, sooner or later, love hurts—usually sooner:

> You were called on account of freedom, brothers; only not a freedom which is a foothold for the flesh; rather through love be slaves to one another. For the whole law has been fulfilled in one word, namely, Love your neighbor as yourself. (Gal 5:13-14)

One of my professors always used this example when he taught about the freedom of love: Imagine two young women coming into a hospital at 7:00 in the morning to visit a very sick man. They stay there all day looking after him. One goes home at 3:00 in the afternoon and the other stays.

Which one is free? We would say that the woman who can go home is free, and the one who has to stay is the slave. We learn later that the one who left was a nurse and the one who stayed was the man's daughter. This information sheds a whole new light on the situation. Wouldn't we then say that the one who stayed and served is free because she is doing what she wants to do out of love for her father?

When we are moved by love, then we are free to serve. *Indeed, the only reason we have been made free is so that we can serve one another.* Find ways to love and serve others. Don't give in to selfishness or fear or ambition. Be willing to become more involved in the lives of others when given the opportunity. Care about your family, care about those close to you, care for those God has given you to love.

If we love and serve others in the power of the Holy Spirit, it will not be exhausting. As St. Augustine said so expansively, "Love knows no fatigue." We will find our strength renewed and our lives enriched as we give to others according to the will of God. As we love freely, peace and unity will follow. Paul exhorted the Ephesians:

> I beseech you, therefore, I, the prisoner in the Lord, to walk worthy of the calling to which you were called, with all humility

and gentleness, with generous patience, bearing with one another in love, being eager to maintain the unity of the Spirit in the bond of peace. (Eph 4:1-3)

Paul is not putting the accent on social graces here. We can learn to act nicely, to be good to people, to be encouraging and good-natured. All of that is certainly better than being mean!

But there is a huge difference between a moral person and a Christian. A *moral* person is someone who acts uprightly as much as he or she can. A *Christian* is someone who knows what Jesus Christ has done for him or her, who loves Jesus Christ and is joined to others in that love.

When we say "yes" to the Lord, we become a "brother" or "sister" in a special way to everyone else who believes in him. Christian love goes so far that we really want to lay down our lives for our brothers and sisters. Husbands and wives are called to lay down their lives for each other every day. Bishops are called to lay down their lives for their flocks every day.

The love that flows from our life in Christ is founded on a whole new reality much deeper than human love:

Rather, being truthful in love, let us in every way grow unto him who is the Head, Christ; from whom the whole Body now being fitted together and brought into connection, through every sustaining juncture according to the effective action, done in the measure of each individual part, is bringing about the growth of this same Body, unto the building up of itself in love. (Eph 4:15-16)

We can't love that way on our own. If the Holy Spirit is not moving us, we can't even understand what "love" means. Unless someone is renewed in the Holy Spirit—unless someone knows that inner power—he or she simply cannot live in unity with other people as the Lord wills it.

Our most important contribution to the restoration of the body of Christ is a personal conversion. Our hearts and minds must be changed and turned toward Christ. Then the Holy Spirit actually changes our hearts so that we see things in a different way. We begin to take on God's perspective, to learn divine wisdom.

Most issues that divide church bodies come from the world, the flesh, and the devil—not from theological problems. If we would dedicate ourselves to prayer and repentance, we would begin to see greater unity among God's people. Paul says to the Philippians,

> So then, if there be any exhortation in Christ, if there be any solace of love, if there be any sharing of the Spirit, if there be any compassion and mercy, make my joy full, in that you think alike having the same love, a single soul, thinking the same thing not with intrigue, not with empty ambition, but in humility thinking others better than yourselves; each one not looking to his own interests but everyone to those of the others. (Phil 2:1-4)

Paul is saying, "If you want me to know that my life has made sense, start to live this way. Then I'll know that the Spirit is truly at work in you and that my life has not been wasted."

The key principle is humility—to consider others better than ourselves. To consider others better is not meant to diminish our own worth.

We should aim to demonstrate our love to others in this way. For example, we can listen to others more respectfully, rather than quickly jumping in with our own opinions. When a friend asks a simple favor of us, we can cheerfully comply because the other is worthy of honor. Jesus Christ died for that person.

Notice the connection in this passage between love and unity. "Strive to have one mind." When you experience difficulty in a relationship, commit yourselves to working it out. The solution is not to shake hands and split: "You have your opinion and I have mine. See you later."

Have you ever been part of a parish torn apart by factions and rivalry? One group believes charismatic prayer isn't right and speaks against the prayer meetings held in the fellowship hall. Another group wants more emphasis to be put on CCD and religious education. Parish council members argue about how to set up a program for evangelization. Others are not happy with the music at the main Sunday liturgy. Satan loves to manipulate these kinds of disputes so that the body of Christ is broken apart.

What is the solution to differences such as these? *Love empowered by the Holy Spirit.* If these factions are allowed to fester, they will tear the parish apart in spirit if not in fact. If people are to worship together, they must work out their difficulties with mutual love and respect.

In a parish situation such as this, the people involved need to abandon their own rigid opinions and pray for a common vision. *"Lord, what is your plan for this parish? Lord, send forth your Holy Spirit to accomplish your purposes here. Lord, help us to love one another more purely."* Prayer is the first avenue in resolving differences: God himself is committed to love and unity in the body of Christ. Then some compromises may need to be made. Perhaps the parish should first pursue the directions upon which they could all agree.

Unselfish love is the key ingredient in unity. God's intention is to have "one Christ loving himself" (St. Augustine). As we understand what this means and are gradually set free from all that holds us in bondage, we will experience new power to love and serve one another.

We are called to lay down our lives for one another. Being a people together for God is founded on the work of the cross—daily dying to sin and yielding to God. In so doing, we unleash the power of love in the world to redeem others, as well as ourselves. When the body of Christ is finally united, the world will really believe that the Father sent the Son.

THAT THE WORLD MAY BELIEVE

The deepest prayer of the Lord is that we may all be perfectly one, so that the world may believe that God sent the Son. Our effectiveness in proclaiming the good news is in direct proportion to our unity, our love and respect for one another. Why should the world believe us if our relationships contradict what we say (see John 17:20-21)?

God abides among us to the extent that we abide in love. Jesus commanded us many times to love one another. Our love for one another reflects our love for God (1 Jn 4:16-21).

If it seems impossible to remain constant in our love for those who share our life in Christ, isn't it astounding that we are further commanded to love even our enemies—those who revile and persecute us?

> If you love those who love you, what credit is that to you? For even sinners love those who love them. And if you do good to those who do good to you, what credit is that to you? For even sinners do the same. And if you lend to those from whom you hope to receive, what credit is that to you? Even sinners lend to sinners, to receive as much again.
>
> But love your enemies, and do good, and lend, expecting nothing in return; and your reward will be great, and you will be sons of the Most High; for he is kind to the ungrateful and the selfish. Be merciful, even as your Father is merciful.
>
> (Lk 6:32-36 RSV)

Jesus illustrated this commandment in the parable of the good Samaritan (Lk 10:30-37). A man traveling from Jerusalem to Jericho was beaten and robbed. Left half dead by the road, his only hope was that someone would have mercy on him. First a priest and then a Levite passed him by on the other side of the road. Perhaps it was the eve of the Sabbath, and they wanted to avoid ritual contamination.

A Samaritan happened to pass by that way soon after. Now the Samaritans were considered by the Jews to be religious heretics and detested even more than pagans. This natural hostility did not stop the Samaritan from having compassion on the Jewish victim. He bound up the wounds of the beaten man, carried him on his own donkey to an inn, and after attending to his needs, left money to repay the innkeeper for any extra expenses.

That Jesus should use a *Samaritan* as an example of love of neighbor was remarkable, even shocking. Through this story, we are taught that the one to whom we are neighbor is anyone in need to whom we show mercy. "Our neighbors" are to include even our enemies.

Jesus is our Good Samaritan. He has shown us the way to love. We were by the side of the road, dying in our sin. The priest and the Levite who passed us by symbolize the law and good works which couldn't save us. But Jesus didn't pass by. He stopped and had compassion on us. We, too, are called to show that same love, with Christ as our model, empowered by his Spirit.

The Holy Spirit is the principal agent of evangelism, and we are called to be his co-workers. By showing love and mercy toward those outside of the body of Christ, we demonstrate the love of God. We draw others to come and know him. God wants us to be hungry for the salvation of souls.

Mother Teresa shows forth such hunger by demonstrating love and mercy to the poorest of the poor and the dying on the street. Every man and woman is her neighbor. In them, she and her sisters see the face of Christ. A few years ago, she opened houses in the United States for AIDS victims, the outcasts of our day.

The Holy Spirit works in signs and wonders to prove the truth about the love of Jesus Christ:

> Now at Lystra there was a man sitting, who could not use his feet; he was a cripple from birth, who had never walked. He listened to Paul speaking; and Paul, looking intently at him and seeing that he had faith to be made well, said in a loud voice, "Stand upright on your feet." And he sprang up and walked.
> (Acts 14:8-10 RSV)

You may not think God can act so dramatically through you, but this same power is available to us. When we proclaim the good news, God himself is committed to proving it true. God wants to impart power to us so that we can show forth his mercy to a dying world.

Boldness to proclaim the good news is based on the joy of knowing where our life is going. What most people want more than anything else is for their lives to make sense. Human beings need some purpose for their existence beyond seeking power or pleasure. We have this knowledge by the anointing of the Holy Spirit.

Unless we know the love of God through Jesus Christ, it makes no sense to work hard all our lives, even to do a lot of good things, only to die. We know what our life is all about. Jesus is the reason we are alive.

In today's world where divorce and family strife are so common, a family knit together by the love of Christ stands out as a dramatic witness to the power of God. A teenager named Bob had been raised in a Christian home. His respect for his father is demonstrated by carefully listening when his father asks him to run an errand, then cheerfully setting aside his studies to obey.

When Bob is invited to a neighborhood party, his father asks him not to go since the teens who live there have a reputation for rowdiness. Rather than grumble and complain, Bob asks his dad if they can do something together instead. Father and son decide to go out for pizza and have a fruitful discussion about Bob's plans for the summer.

When the body of Christ allows the work of God to go on in its midst, then people have to say, "There really is a living God. Look at their lives. Look at their families. Look at the obedience of their children. Look at the meaning in their lives. Look at the way they are not afraid of the things that make us afraid. Who has done this for them?"

When we grasp who God is and what he has done for us, we are filled with joy. If you were walking across thin ice and fell through, you would yell for help. Suppose you are going down for the third time, and somebody grabs you and saves you. You wouldn't say, "Well, I don't want to get emotional about this, but thank you very much." You would know what someone has just done for you—saved you from dying in the icy water.

God has saved us from eternal death. Jesus Christ has saved us. Our joy should freely spill over onto the lives of those who need to hear the good news. We should want to share with them the best thing that we have—knowing Jesus.

THE HOPE OF HEAVEN

This unity of love, which is the ultimate mission of the church, will find its complete fulfillment in heaven. There we will be perfectly one with God and all of our brothers and sisters. It is that realization and hope that can help sustain us when the going gets rough here below. The hope of heaven gives us the motivation and eternal perspective to continue our earthly pilgrimage.

The ultimate work of the Holy Spirit is to lead us to dwell with the Father forever. Through obedience to the Son of God, we can begin to enter into the kingdom of heaven here on earth. We have been blessed with "every spiritual blessing in the heavenly realm" (Eph 1:3).

The blessing is spiritual. Paul is speaking of that heavenly realm beyond the limits of fallen human existence, which nevertheless acts upon us. Through the Holy Spirit, we now have access to that realm.

> But God, being rich in mercy, because of his great love with which he loved us, we ourselves being dead in our transgressions, brought us to life with Christ—by grace you are [in the state of having been] saved—and raised us up with him, and seated us with him in the heavenly realm in Christ Jesus, so that he might demonstrate in the ages to come the surpassing wealth of his grace in his kindness toward us in Christ Jesus.
>
> (Eph 2:4-7)

What a glorious vision! In Christ, we can enter the place where God reigns, where ultimate decisions are made. In Christ, we will inherit immeasurable riches of grace, worth far more than gold and diamonds.

The Holy Spirit wants to make known to us the hope to which we are called and the riches of our inheritance. He wants to give us a heavenly vision—an eternal perspective to encourage and strengthen us in hard times.

Sometimes the veil is lifted and we are able to catch a glimpse of heaven: "what no eye has seen, nor ear heard, nor the heart of man conceived, what God has prepared for those who love him" (1 Cor 2:9 RSV). John received such a revelation:

> And I saw a new heaven and a new earth. For the first heaven and the first earth passed away, and the sea is no longer. And I saw the holy city, new Jerusalem, coming down from heaven, from God, made ready like a bride adorned for her husband. And I heard a great voice from the throne saying: Behold the dwelling of God with men, and he will dwell with them and they will be his people and God himself will be with them as their God. And he will wipe away every tear from their eyes, and death will be no more; neither mourning, nor weeping, nor pain will be any more; the old order passed away. (Rv 21:1-4)

This happiness of heaven is hard to comprehend. Each of us tends to picture that joy in terms of the sorrows we now experience. The poor man, for instance, looks forward to a release from his toil and poverty in a place which offers an abundance of all that he craves.

The woman who has suffered a lifelong disease looks forward to release from intense physical pain in a place of perpetual health.

The man who has been severely buffeted his whole life by strong temptations from the devil, the world, and his own flesh, looks forward to heaven as a place where temptation and sin shall be no more.

The woman who has been emotionally torn apart by broken relationships looks forward to a release from tears in a place where the heart knows only love.

All of these longings will be satisfied. But the essential joy of heaven comes from dwelling with God. When we behold the beauty of God himself in the fullness of his glory, then all the former things will pass away. Then, finally, we will no longer need the counsel of the Holy Spirit, for we will be fully alive—fully ourselves in Christ.

God knows the deepest longings of the human heart. He is continually speaking to us of his love, if we would only open our hearts and ears to hear. He holds out to us a life that is unbelievably glorious and magnificent. Even in the weakness of our flesh, we can begin to know the power that is at work in us—the same power that raised Jesus from the dead.

God begs us to receive the glorious inheritance reserved for us in Christ. He sends forth the Holy Spirit into our hearts so that we will know him. When we abide in his Son Jesus, then we will know the length, breadth, height, and depth of God's love for each one of us—the love that passes all understanding.

God has given us the pledge of eternal life in the Holy Spirit. He is the living, fiery Flame of Love who dwells within us: the Father of the poor, the greatest Consoler, the most knowledgeable Counselor, the loving Guest of our soul. The Holy Spirit has already begun in us that work which will be completed when, by the light of glory, our minds are so strengthened that we can gaze upon God. We already possess a foretaste of that light, we can know the power of the Holy Spirit as he brings to birth in our lives the power of the death and resurrection of Jesus Christ.

Turn now to God, the Father, and seek his face. Beg him to send forth his light and his truth, his Holy Spirit, who will bring you to know in a way unmistakable that Jesus Christ is the Lord. As Paul has already written (2 Cor 4:6): "For the same God who said: 'Out of darkness let light shine,' has caused his light to shine within us, to give the light of revelation—the revelation of the glory of God in the face of Jesus Christ."

Afterword

CHANGE IS THE SUREST SIGN OF LIFE. For example, consider the incredible changes that occur in our lives as human beings from birth to eighteen years of age. We are born utterly helpless and vulnerable, completely dependent upon our parents for food, clothing, and shelter. Yet a mere eighteen years later our bodies and minds are hopefully ready to assume the responsibilities of adulthood. At least that is the working assumption of the state in declaring us legally of age at eighteen and holding us responsible for our actions as adults.

Our own experience of the changes which the Holy Spirit brings about in us provides an unmistakable indication of God's presence with us. It also gives us a firm assurance of the goal to which he is leading us—a glorious new life in Christ which will not fade and die. Just as our Lord Jesus Christ is the "one who came," that is, the one who accomplished the whole work of salvation, so the Holy Spirit is the "one who bears witness" (see 1 John 5:7). The Spirit bears witness by bringing us to new life in the power of the cross and strengthening our minds. Thus, we are empowered to participate in the ongoing revelation of God's saving plan as it is being realized in and through the church in each generation. That is exciting, good news for each of us!

What I have said in *The Life-Changer* can be summarized in two key points that describe this life-changing process in us: 1) God is at work in our age in a particular way, renewing minds so that we are aware of him and able to turn to him; and 2) our initial reception of this grace must be followed by an ongoing action of the Holy Spirit by which the power of the cross of Christ is applied to our lives in order to change them and give us an ever greater ability to live our new life in Christ.

Let me conclude this book by saying a few words about each of these points.

BECOMING AWARE OF GOD

The greatest crisis of our age is the lack of the awareness of God. Walter Kasper, a German theologian and now a bishop, has expressed the state of the modern mind with keen insight:

> In this secularized world God becomes increasingly super-fluous as a hypothesis for explaining phenomena within the world; he loses his function in regard to the world. We must live in the world "as though there were no God." Thus faith in God becomes increasingly emptied of its perceptual and exper-iential elements and increasingly unreal; God himself becomes increasingly unreal. When all is said and done, the statement "God is dead" could serve as a plausible interpretation of the modern sense of life and reality. (*The God of Jesus Christ* [tr.] Matthew J. O'Connell [New York: Crossroad Publishing Co., 1987], p. 10)

This lack of awareness of God has penetrated into the church as well. The lack of "perceptual and experiential elements" in faith has made God "increasingly unreal," even among many baptized and confirmed Catholics who fill our church pews each Sunday. So many are loyal to God and to the church, but they find themselves helpless when it comes to being aware of God as the center of their lives—the source of meaning for themselves and the basis of their authority when speaking with their children.

The great outpouring of the Holy Spirit which has characterized our century is an important part of God's response to this dilemma of his people. How many Christians have been brought to an awareness of God through some dramatic happening in their lives? For many it was an experience by which they became aware of the reality and care of God in their lives. Through a physical or emotional healing, through a life-changing encounter with Christ at a retreat or weekend, or in some other way, "God" became more than a concept. He became a personal Father. Jesus became much more than a great figure of the past; he became the living and present Lord.

All of this is the work of the holy and divine Spirit who is present in a new way in the world because Jesus has been glorified (see John 7:37-39). The Spirit, poured out under the symbol of water from the side of Christ (Jn 19:34), is the one who "bears witness" by distributing the manifold grace won for humanity by the death of the Lord Jesus Christ. A number of the examples in this book have demonstrated the powerful, life-changing work of this grace.

How has this action of God been experienced in this mighty move of the Spirit? For some, the charismatic gifts, destined by God for the building of the body of Christ, achieved their first effect by building the faith of those who possessed and practiced them. People were delivered from their alienation and loneliness and given the joy of being aware of God.

COMING TO A KNOWLEDGE OF GOD

However, there is more. We are called by God not only to be aware of him, but to *know* him. Experience of God on an emotional and perceptual level is indispensable, but it is not enough. This experience may be compared to knowing the sacraments only on an external level, involving the senses. A sacrament is the action of Christ in the church accomplished through a sign which symbolizes and points to a deep work of God in a person, brought about through the faith that it stirs up. What would happen, for instance, if we were to stop at the experience of being washed clean by the baptismal waters or being fed by the Eucharist, and were not to go on by faith to lay hold of what these sensible signs are pointing to? The whole purpose of the sacrament would be frustrated. Compare that to the description St. Cyprian gave of his own baptism! (See page 53).

Most of this book has been devoted to helping people understand how God is calling them to pass from an awareness of him to a growing knowledge of him. I defined baptism in the Holy Spirit as a grace of revelation (see Ephesians 1:7) by which the Holy Spirit confers on the spirit of the believer a living and conscious faith knowledge of the reality and majesty of Jesus Christ, the eternal

Son of God and risen Savior of the world.

The first stirrings of this grace, often in a dramatic moment, do not confer its fullness. At this privileged moment, the "perceptual and experiential" elements of faith are restored in such a way that everything can be seen anew. This is a visible sign of an invisible grace. Jesus is revealed for who he really is, but the revelation is as yet only in its beginning stages.

To use some illustrations, a seed has truly been planted, something new is present in the person's life, but the full potential of this grace has yet to be exploited by our cooperation with the action of the Holy Spirit in our lives. It is early springtime in God's mysterious cycle of grace, new life, maturity, death, and resurrection. As I said in chapter six, we cannot, on our own resources, journey to the place where this grace will mature to fullness, but we can "cling to the horse." We can lay hold of the action of the Holy Spirit and obey him in our daily lives.

There are many ways of describing the journey from awareness of the Lord to knowledge of him. We may speak of the difference between an "enlightened mind" and a "transformed mind" as I did in chapter five. We may speak of being conscious of the "symbolic" or "sacramental" nature of our initial experience of new life as opposed to our need to personally assimilate that revelation of God's mysterious action, made once for all to the whole church and now alive within us.

In these and other descriptions, we become acutely aware of the power we lack in ourselves to bring about such a transformation. We recognize our need for the power of the cross of Jesus Christ. What do I mean by the power of the cross? It is the infinite, dynamic energy of that supreme, human act of love performed by the Second Person of the Trinity which took place at the moment of Jesus' death. It is both the source of the transformation of his own humanity at the resurrection and the reason why he is now "the source of an eternal salvation for all who obey him" (Heb 5:9).

We sing in the Preface of the Passion: "The power of the cross reveals your judgment on this world and the kingship of Christ crucified." As the Holy Spirit applies the power of the cross to our lives, this revelation becomes real to us. In God's rhythm of grace and new life, we enter into Christ's death that we might have a share in his glorious resurrection. We start to understand how the Holy Spirit proves the world to be wrong in regard to sin, justice, and judgment (Jn 16:7-11; see p. 142). We know personally the royal authority of Jesus as he gives us the ability to take authority over our lives—even to the point of overcoming bad habits and patterns of sin that have plagued us for years.

There are two aspects, or perhaps effects, of the Holy Spirit's activity in our lives by which he makes real his witness to us of the power of the cross. As the words of the preface imply, first, we experience a freedom from the power of sin. Second, as a result of this, we grow in an abiding, personal knowledge of the Son of God.

How is this freedom from the power of sin achieved? We saw that the act of love in which Jesus died was the act by which he died to sin (Rom 6:10). Sin is that malevolent power of self-love and rebellion against God which exists personified in Satan. It entered the world "through one man," causing death, estrangement from God, to spread out to "all people" (Rom 5:12). We are baptized into that act of love when, by the act of Christ in and through his body, the church, we are baptized into his very death (Rom 6:3). Thus, we are to realize that now we, too, are "dead to Sin, but alive to God in Christ Jesus" (Rom 6:11). We have moved out from under the domination of the structures of sin to live already in the "glorious freedom of the children of God" (Rom 8:21). A large portion of this book has described how we are called to cooperate with this action of the Holy Spirit by a continual process of letting go of our connivance in sin and letting our habit patterns of sin be put to death.

What of our abiding, personal knowledge of the Son of God? This takes place along with our growing freedom from the power of sin. It is precisely the journey from awareness of the Lord to knowledge of him. There is a saying in theology that "God is known in his effects." This is true not only of the splendid created universe, of which we are a part and which we see all around us, but also of the work of grace in our own lives. Our death to sin and consequent experience of freedom from its former work in us is an experience of the power of God, that power "at work in us believers" by which he raised Christ from the dead (see Ephesians 1:19-20).

It is because of this unmistakable effect in our lives that we gain a personal knowledge of God, based on our experience of freedom from the habit patterns of sin. As we move out from bondage, the "eyes of our heart are enlightened" (Eph 1:18) and the Spirit produces in us that divine affection for God the Father (Abba) by which the Spirit becomes the "pledge" of our eternal inheritance (see Ephesians 1:14). No words can express the inner joy and sweetness of this knowledge of the Lord. To whatever degree we come to possess it, this knowledge becomes the one really precious pearl of human life, so much so that it makes sense to trade everything in order to have it.

THE WITNESS OF LOVE AND A CHANGED LIFE

The beautiful words of St. Augustine which open chapter one are witness to how such a gracious work of God in Christ, through the action of the Spirit, becomes a source of meaning and joy beyond our imagination. It is the result of that strengthening of the mind I spoke about in chapter five. Or let us listen to St. Thomas as he describes the visit of the Son of God, divine Wisdom. He is speaking about the fact that we come to knowledge of the Son in and through the grace of his manifestation to us, which is a work of the Holy Spirit:

> The Son is the Word, not just any word, but one that breathes forth love. So St. Augustine says, "The Word about which I am speaking is knowledge accompanied by love." So then, not just any perfection of the mind constitutes a sending of the Son but only that enlightening that bursts forth into love. As John says, "Everyone who has heard from the Father, and learned, comes to me" (Jn 6:45); and the Psalm says, "In my meditation, a fire will blaze forth" (Ps 39:4). So Augustine explicitly says, "The Son is sent when he is known or perceived by someone." The word "perception" signifies a certain experiential knowledge and this precisely is what wisdom is: a knowing that is as it were, a "tasting." (*Summa Theologiae*, 1, 43, 5, 2).

From the very initial stages of God's work in our lives, we are made aware of him. This means that the Son has been sent in some way into our lives. If we apply this to baptism in the Holy Spirit, which is the revelation of Jesus, we can see that this rudimentary perception—as precious as it is—only reaches maturity in that kind of intimate knowledge of his reality and majesty which bursts forth into love.

This is the preeminent fruit of the Holy Spirit. Such a love is a response to God first of all, but it includes within itself love for all those whom God has created and loves. It even reaches out to embrace those we consider our enemies! God's love in us is a force borne of the power of the cross and takes root as sin is put to death. This is the basis for an experiential knowledge of the plan of salvation as it matures in our lives and bears fruit. This is what I meant by saying that our lives are like a laboratory where we work with the divine truths and come to know them personally. Or we could describe our lives as part of the vine which is Christ, growing under the care of the master gardener.

When the gospel is preached out of such personal knowledge, it is carried out "in power and in the Holy Spirit and with full conviction" (1 Thes 1:5 RSV). It is at this point that the Lord's intent in baptizing us in the Holy Spirit is fully realized. In the power of this new conviction, we can proclaim with confidence the plan God has for the salvation of the world and be the means of bringing people to share it. We can embody this plan and make it real to people by showing forth the care God has for humankind "especially the poor or those who are afflicted in any way" (*Gaudium et Spes*, #1). The world is hungry for bread, for peace, for a sense of dignity and direction. The world needs to know salvation and see it realized already in a sacramental and prophetic way that points to the end of the age. The Lord has responded by making some of us aware of him and, if we are faithful, leading us to know him intimately.

This is the witness the world so desperately needs. The world doesn't ultimately need a proliferation of more "things" and programs to solve its problems. The witness the world is really waiting for is that of a changed life, that of a heart that has been transformed and is no longer a heart of stone but a human heart. This sharing in the heart of Christ enables us to love and trust God, and even to embrace the suffering of the world, holding it up to God and reaching out to lift this heavy burden off the backs of those it nearly crushes. In this way, the world will finally know that our God is a living God who is near to all who call on him.

The final question *The Life-Changer* poses then is unmistakably clear: Are you happy with your life as it is? Or do you want the Spirit to change you into the fragrance of Christ to a winter-weary world yearning for spring?

Other Books of Interest
from Servant Publications

Simplicity
by John Michael Talbot

The good news is: you don't necessarily have to do more or less to live simply, because simplicity starts with an inner attitude of humility and obedience to God. You can renounce every material possession and still miss it. You can fast vigorously and perform other spiritual disciplines, yet still miss it.

In the clear light of simplicity, John Michael Talbot shows you how areas like prayer, self-discipline, food, clothing, shelter, and works of mercy can all take their proper place—bringing spiritual freedom into your life. Discover how simplicity can change the way you think and live—every day. *$7.95*

The Truth about Trouble
by Michael Scanlan, T.O.R.

It's been one of those days.... You've just missed your prayer and Scripture devotions for the third time running. And you just lost your temper again. You remember the "good old days" when God seemed so close and life seemed much easier. Where is God, anyway, when you really need him?

The truth is God hasn't moved, and you may be right where he can help you most—in trouble! That's the surprisingly good news Fr. Michael Scanlan shares in his new book. When you turn your troubles over to Jesus Christ, your everyday problems can lead to deeper maturity and intimacy with God. *$6.95*